The One Room Schoolhouse:

Morgan County, Colorado

On the Cover:
Twombly School, Brush Colo. (1915)
Image courtesy of the Library of Congress

The One Room Schoolhouse:

Morgan County, Colorado

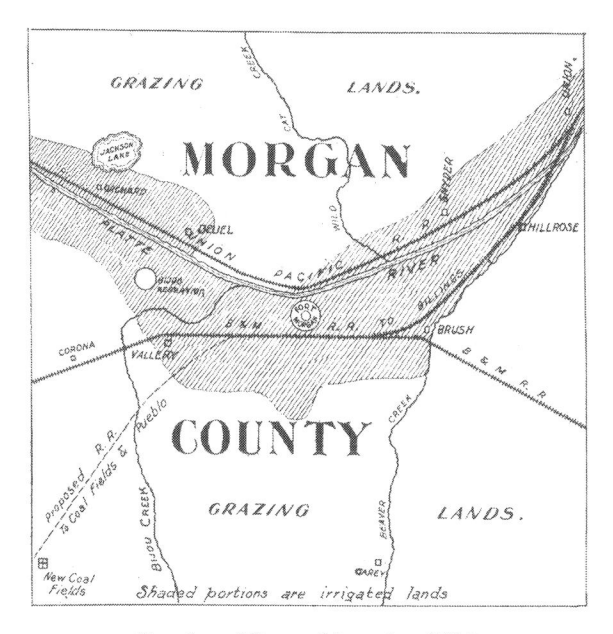

Ranch and Range Magazine (1902)

Brian C. Mack Ed.

THE FORT MORGAN HERITAGE FOUNDATION

Library of Congress Number
(LCCN): 2016915100

ISBN-13: 978-1537574288
ISBN-10: 1537574280

All rights reserved. No part of this book shall be reproduced, stored in an information retrieval system, or transmitted in any form or by any means, mechanical or electrical, photocopied or recorded, without the express written consent of the Fort Morgan Heritage Foundation and without full and proper written acknowledgment of the editor.

The information contained in THE ONE ROOM SCHOOLHOUSE: MORGAN COUNTY, COLORADO is believed to be accurate at the time of printing, but no representation or warranty is given express or implied as to its accuracy, completeness or correctness. The editor shall not accept any liability whatsoever for any direct, indirect or consequential loss or damage arising in any way from any use of or reliance on this material for any purpose.

THE ONE ROOM
SCHOOLHOUSE: MORGAN
COUNTY, COLORADO
First Published in 2016
Fort Morgan, CO
Printed in the U.S.A.
Copyright ©2016

For Thelma Downing and David Roberts
whose years of research, on-site exploration,
and photography made this book possible.

Thelma Downing
Ghost Children Sharing Memories
16" x 20" oil on canvas
Image Courtesy of Thelma Downing

Globe
Image Courtesy of the Library of Congress

TABLE OF CONTENTS

Dedication v
List of Illustrations viii
Foreword ix
Acknowledgements xi
Introduction 1

I. The Rural One-Room School Building 3

II. Teachers of One Room Schools — The Early Years 9

III. Students, Deportment (Behavior) 13

IV. Teacher Contracts 15

V. Experiences of Helen Underwood 17

VI. A Day In the Life of Teacher and Student 19

VII. Experiences of Thelma (Kentopp) Downing 21

VII. School Yard Games 23

VIII. Moving School Houses 25

IX. Tragedy at North Star School 27

X. Survey of Morgan County One Room Schools 29
    Map: Morgan County One Room Schools 32-33

XI. Recently Discovered Rural Schools 119

XII. The End of Rural Schools 123

Afterword 124
Appendix 1: List of Morgan County Superintendents 126
Appendix 2: Popular One Room School Games 127
Bibliography 128
Index 130

LIST OF ILLUSTRATIONS

Morgan County iii
Ghost Children v
Globe vi
Abraham Lincoln xii
Morgan County 2
Morgan County Atlas 5
North Prairie Style School 6
Ambrose School Interior 7
School No. 9 District No. 3 8
School No. 9 District No. 3 (2) 11
Horseback to School 12
Teacher's Contract 14
Teacher—Lura Elkerton 15
Unknown Morgan County School.. 18
Baseball at Victory School 23
Oxen at Weldon Valley 24
Musgrave Homestead 24
Fort Morgan Times 26
Helen Mura Gravesite 26
Old Trail School 28
Fort Morgan, Colo. 30-31
Atlas 32-33
Adena School 36
Adena School II 37
Adena School c. 1920 38-39
Adena School (newest) 40
Sod School House 40
Ambrose School 41
Antelope Bend 42
Antelope Springs 43
Antelope Valley 44
Bijou View 46
Brammer 47
Centerville 49
Report Card 50
Colwell School 51
Fairview 53
Grant School 54-55
Garfield School 56

Gilliland School 58
Glenwood School 60
Goodrich School 61-62
Hoyt School 66
Light School 69
Knearl School 70-71
Long Meadow School 72
Morey School 75
N.E. Gary 76
North Star School 78
School Picnic 78
O'Dell 79
OK School 80
Old Trail School 81
Adena Sod Interior 82
Orchard School 82
Orchard Sod School 83
Orchard School House 84-85
Paul School 87
Peace Valley 88
State Teacher's Diploma............ 90-91
Riverside 93
San Arroyo School 95
Snyder School 96
Sunnyside School...................... 98
Unknown School Interior 99-100
Twombly School 102
Hurd Warren Twombly 102
Union School 103
Upper Wildcat 104
Report Card for King 106
Victory School 107
Weldona School 109
Wiggins School on an Outing ... 108-109
Wiggins School Bus 110
Williams School 114
Facsimile of Research Paper.......... 118
Della Brown School 119
Fort Morgan Middle school 122

vi

FOREWARD

The Fort Morgan Heritage Foundation is pleased to publish this history of the one-room schools in Morgan County. The new settlers in our county knew that our successful democracy depended on an educated citizenry and an informed electorate. These early settlers made the availability of public schools for our children a priority. This meant acquiring land on which to build, structure specifications, and funds to build the often, tiny buildings. Once built, finding teachers willing to live in rural areas to staff the schools must have been a challenge.

The researchers were most innovative in using Google Earth Imaging to zoom into the sites of the old schools. From space cameras orbiting the earth, we can see foundations, imprints of playgrounds, cisterns, and trails leading to the schools. Through county courthouse records, we know precisely the locations as seen from space that allow us to actually examine the remnants on the ground.

Membership in the Fort Morgan Heritage Foundation is open to everyone. A governing board consisting of 17 volunteers meets monthly to assist the Fort Morgan Museum staff to assist in charting the course of the museum programs, publications and exhibits. The proceeds from the sale of this book benefit the Fort Morgan Heritage Foundation.

Donald A. Ostwald Sr.
President,
Fort Morgan Heritage Foundation

Thanks to the various members of the Community History Writers whose contributions helped make this book possible.

ACKNOWLEDGEMENTS

As a community Morgan County has a fascinating history, and we are delighted to be able to shed a light on the educational history that has helped to make this community so rich. While this book contains only a shadow of everything that has made Morgan County so special, we hope that readers are able to get a sense of the community we have long considered to be home. Compiling the information contained in this book was a rewarding work of intrigue. This endeavor could not have been completed without the assistance of the following contributors: Walter Barrett, Thelma Downing, Kat Dupre, City of Fort Morgan, The Fort Morgan Heritage Foundation, Chandra McCoy, Karen Morgan, Lanny Page, David Roberts, and McKinley Thompson.

Recognition to Lloyd Ladd and Bob Lumpkin for their work on the 1976 County Schools map, and the Morgan County Commissioners for permission to use the their research.

Unless otherwise noted, all images are courtesy of the Fort Morgan Museum.

*The philosophy of the school room in one generation
will be the philosophy of government in the next.*

Abraham Lincoln (1809—1865)

Image courtesy of Library of Congress

INTRODUCTION

"School days, school days, dear old golden rule days, readin' and ritin', arithmetic, taught to the tune of a hickory stick." The historic rural "country" school houses throughout Colorado and the western United States were much more than the 3-R's to students and parents. They served as focal points for a multitude of business, social and academic needs of the community. Primarily, though, they provided as many as six generations of students with that solid foundation of useful knowledge and learning upon which they built their lives.

The "Prairie Schools" in Morgan County, Colorado, and elsewhere, were a product of the Homestead Act of 1862 which opened the American West with the promise of virtually free land. Now, 154 years later, almost all of the thousands of homestead schools across the west have disappeared, and, except for the very few that have been deliberately preserved in their original form, almost all of those that are still standing, have been incorporated into homes or modern buildings. Most schools have fallen into ruin.

Before 1889, Morgan County did not exist. Weld County extended from its western borders with Larimer and Boulder Counties to the Kansas State Line. All of the schools in that huge expanse of high prairie were Weld County schools. Then, by an 1889 Act of the Colorado Legislature, thirty-six townships in southeastern Weld County were taken to form a new county named "Morgan County." Eight School Districts were then created to serve the education needs of its residents.

W. E. Garver was elected first County Superintendent of Schools. According to the census of 1890, there were 359 school-age children housed in nine buildings throughout the newly defined school districts. The County Superintendent supervised and directed the schools and helped the local School Board find, hire and fire teachers, and the superintendent was expected to visit the schools at least twice a year and prepare reports, and almost always showed up unannounced. One can imagine how the teacher, caught off-guard, felt as she became greatly concerned with how the students might recite, how they would do their lessons, and how they would behave and perform during the Superintendent's presence.

Morgan County (1915)
Image courtesy of Library of Congress

I.

THE RURAL ONE-ROOM SCHOOL BUILDING

The first one-room schools were held in dugouts or in a structures built of prairie sod. On a few occasions, school was held in an abandoned house. As time passed, the rural schools in Morgan County progressed to real school buildings made of concrete, lumber, and materials shipped by rail to the nearest rail town.

Schools were often moved from section to section as needed, to more effectively serve the scattered school-age children. In fact, some of the smaller schools were built on skids to make moving easier. As the population of children moved, so did their school. Reports tell us that schools were moved using teams of horses, and that a relocated school was often re-named at its new site.

A school and its outbuildings were ordinarily set on one or two acres of land, usually granted or leased to the District by the landowner, and, often for that reason, the school was named for the landowner. When a school closed and was removed, ownership of the land typically reverted back to the landowner.

In 1976 Lloyd Ladd and Bob Lumpkin officially surveyed Morgan County to identify and locate its rural schools. They prepared a detailed map identifying and locating ninety-six school sites. Unfortunately, the names of some of the schools, even then, were lost to history, and because they were moveable, the actual number of buildings remains unknown. A unique 1913 Atlas by Geo. A. Ogle & Co. of Chicago, Illinois, was also made available by the Jolliffe family of Fort Morgan as an additional resource to locate schools. There were forty-four Morgan County schools in 1913 when the Atlas was published.

What did the "country school" look like? Typically the school grounds of an acre including one or two outhouses, a shed for fuel, sometimes a cellar, a water well or cistern, and a shed for horses ridden or driven to school. In some cases, for lack of water, cisterns were built and water was hauled to the school by a tanker wagon, or later by a truck. A few of the remote schools included a "teacherage" provided by the District to house the teacher, but many, if not most, of the teachers found room and board with the family of one or more of the teacher's students or with close-by residents.

Most of the schools contained a vestibule or entrance porch in which coats were hung and lunch pails stored. Drinking water was kept there in a large crock as the source of water for washing and drinking, most often by use of a common dipper or ladle and shallow wash pan. Inside the main room were desks lined in a row; the smallest desks in front and larger ones to the back. The stove was often in the middle of the room with space for desks around it. The front of the room contained a platform upon which the teacher's desk sat, and sometimes there was a piano.

Behind the teacher's desk there was usually a wall cabinet, a paddle, a large pull-down set of maps, and, of course, a United States flag. Typically a portrait of George Washington graced one of the side walls. If they were available, slate blackboards were attached to the remaining walls.

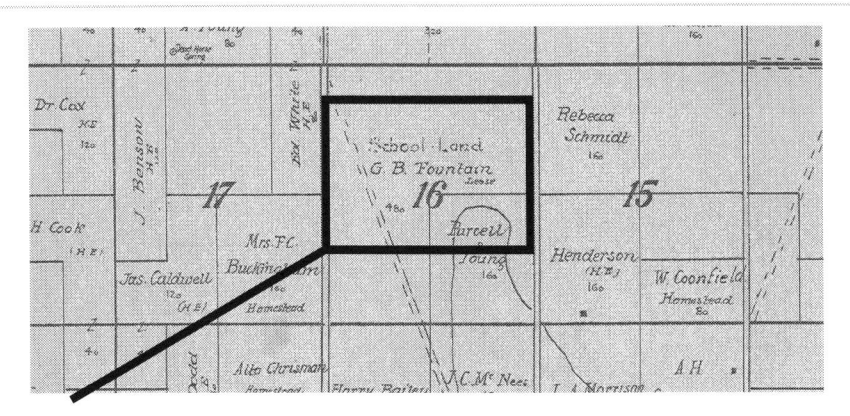

1913 Morgan County Atlas shows an example of a School Land Section

School books were shelved on or near the teacher's desk. Books of various kinds were provided by the school district, by parents, and by residents.

In the early years, schools were in session for three to five months because the children were needed to work the farm. As the years progressed the school term was extended to six months and then, eventually, to nine months. Over the years, the average kindergarten through eighth grade enrollment in Morgan County's rural schools was twenty students.

Throughout the year, the schoolhouse served as a sort of community center for public meetings including: Christmas pageants, spelling bees, pie suppers, and a host of other meetings. Kerosene or "coal oil" lamps were provided to light the evening gatherings. It was said: "There was a distinctive aroma in these buildings reminiscent of chalk dust, sweeping compound, lunches of several years, and pencil sharpener shavings."

There were two major varieties of schools: the South Prairie Style and the North Prairie style. Adopting one or the other style was determined largely by climate and the availability of building materials. Typically, rural school houses in Morgan County were of the North Prairie style — made of lumber and incorporated a steeply pitched roof to shed the snow.

Example of a North Prairie style schoolhouse—
Ambrose School (see page 41)
(1916)

In the early days teachers were sometimes as young as sixteen years old with no formal training. The one-room school teacher was classified as a third class teacher. Later aspiring teachers were offered "Normal Training" classes in High School (Persell 104). This was a two year concentrated course in all the techniques of teaching as well as familiarity with the subject matter to be taught (Persell 124). In 1952 a teacher had to attend summer school receiving 12 hours of college credit or 90 quarter hours (one year) at a college. Elementary certificates had to be renewed every three years by attending summer school sessions at a college. *The Course of Study*, published by the State Education Department, was the guide placed in schools for the teachers. This book covered grades one through eight and outlined all subjects and materials that were to be taught at each grade level. This was truly a life-saver for any teacher, and as the result of this standardization, each student was provided the opportunity to obtain an approved standard education.

Ambrose School Interior

Before the County of Morgan was carved out of territory originally allocated to Weld County, School Superintendent Packard, on February 19, 1889, organized the Weld County School District No. 4 to serve the Brush community. After Morgan County was formed by an Act of the Legislature on May 8, 1883, the Brush District No. 1 application was accepted. Brush became District No. 2. Snyder became District No. 1 on April 22, 1883, and Fort Morgan became District No. 3 on August 8, 1884.

School No. 9 District No. 3 — Morgan County (1915)
Image courtesy of the Library of Congress

II.

TEACHERS OF ONE-ROOM SCHOOLS
THE EARLY YEARS

The first teacher's examination in Morgan County was held at the Office of County Superintendent on May 31, 1890. A typical teacher test was administered over a period of two days, and was designed to comprehensively test the candidate's knowledge of all academic subjects to be taught.

Typically, sixty to eighty percent of the rural school teachers were women. In that day, women teachers were most often young, unmarried, and expected to serve their community as the personification of "wisdom and virtue." She was also expected to pass on those qualities to her students. In the early years, many teachers were teenagers prepared to teach by Normal Training Classes taught in high school. Classes were offered as a course of study during two high school years. Standard teaching techniques, as well as the essentials of the subject matter, were taught. Some would-be teachers might have been required to take college courses for as little as one summer, or maybe for a single year, to become qualified for their renewable, three-year Class Three Teacher Certificate.

Rural schools were, most often, unavoidably isolated. The nearest neighbor might be several miles away. Of course, early on, there were no telephones, no automobiles, or any sort of help readily available. In case of an emergency, the teacher of the day, necessarily, had to be a resourceful sort of person. Stories from *My Folks and the One Room Schoolhouse* include:

> ... teachers observed riding horses or driving buggies across huge pastures ... of a lady teacher carrying a gun on her side and knowing how to use it ... of a model T Ford bumping along on crude roads and double-track trails ... of a lady teacher riding a bike having to stop all too often to fix her tires ... of a teacher breaking through snow on foot, sometimes so deep that walking was nearly impossible ... of a teacher having to somehow learn to communicate in the foreign language of her immigrant students and their parents with a proper regard for their customs ... and often of the need to become reconciled to living so remotely that a visit to one's family was possible only twice during the school year.

In the days of the 1930's, the dust was so heavy in the air that sometimes one could not see the road or path in front of them, or breathe without something over the face. Some teachers faced teaching in sod houses which seemed to be regularly available to snakes, rats, and mice. School was often held in abandoned houses. Often paper and crayon served for a blackboard. Nowadays it is difficult to imagine the teacher living with a family of five in their one room home with just a curtain for her own bedroom privacy.

Available written accounts, from various sources provide many amusing and some not so amusing accounts of actual events in the lives of teachers in the country schools. For instance:

> ... there is the tale of a first grader who threw-up all over the teacher and the desk during the very first day he went to school ... of a mother telling the teacher not to remove

School No. 9 District No. 3 — Morgan County (1915)
Image courtesy of the Library of Congress

the red yarn around Johnny's neck as it kept him from getting a nosebleed . . . of the teacher who was startled by a huge owl when she opened the door to the coal stove . . .

of rats jumping out of desk drawers . . . of ants and wasps in outhouses, and bees inside the walls of the school . . . of a bull at the front door, and pigs and chickens in the schoolyard to gather up scraps from the children's lunches . . . of a trap set for a mouse which caught a skunk . . . and the story of a tramp who spent a night in the school house . . . of a tornado alert and the run to the nearest ditch . . . or dealing with a flooded creek . . . and a teacher's description of the scent of wet clothes from a walk in the snow or rain, or that polite description of the distinct odor originating on a winter's day from all the un-bathed bodies in a heated school room.

George, Kay, and John Glenn rode horseback to the OK School
(see page 80). They rode the horse named Sikes.
Earlier George and Kay rode a Shetland pony named Queenie,
but she was not large enough to carry all three children. (1945)
Image courtesy of the Glenn Family Collection

III

STUDENT'S DEPORTMENT (BEHAVIOR)

Recorded accounts of teachers and others assure us that rural students were mostly well behaved and loved their schooling. It is well known, however, that not all students were there just to learn. In many of the schools, boys were, quite often, bigger than the teacher, and they sometimes saw it as their mission to intimidate or "run off" the teacher — whether a "ma'am" or a "sir."

There is an account of several school boys who had successfully "run-off" two young lady teachers in one year, so a male teacher was hired. The boys soon won his confidence and persuaded him to join in their outside games. One day in the course of playing hide-and-seek, teacher was coaxed into a wood shed. The boys immediately locked the door; the teacher was not let out until going-home-time at four o'clock.

Typical of other pranks were to catch the teacher in the outside toilet and lock the door to enjoy a longer recess. Another incident involved purposefully stuffing the chimney with straw so when a fire was started, the school filled with smoke. On Halloween, an outhouse placed against the front door of a school would keep the teacher out for awhile. We know that it is true that spit balls were a sport for years and dipping a girl's long braid in the ink bottle was, indeed, done. Many more pranks were mentioned in those written accounts, adding, of course, that many were suitably and routinely dealt with, as a paddle or a hickory stick was most always near to hand, and they were there to be used. Their purpose was, of course, to avoid a disservice to the child implicit in the widespread belief that "to spare the rod is to spoil the child." It was also suggested that when recently disciplined students arrived home from school, quite often a second round of discipline awaited them.

Teacher's Contract.

Section 11, Subdivision 4.—School Laws.

This Agreement, Entered into this 29 day of June, 1907, between School District No. 103, of Gage County, Nebraska, and Mattie Martin, a qualified teacher of said County,

Witnesseth, That the said Mattie Martin agrees to teach the school of said District in a faithful and efficient manner for the term of seven months, commencing on the 2nd day of Sept., 1907, and agrees to keep herself qualified, and agrees in all things to observe the rules and regulations of the District Board. And to do her own janitor work

In Consideration Whereof, said School District agrees to pay said Teacher the sum of $35.00 per month for said services, and agrees to keep the school house in good repair; to provide the necessary fuel and supplies, and to furnish janitor work.

Provided, that in case said Mattie Martin shall be discharged for sufficient cause by the District Board, or shall have her certificate annulled, she shall not be entitled to any compensation from and after such dismissal or annulment.

In Witness Whereof, We have hereunto subscribed our names this Third day of September A. D. 1907

APPROVED:

H. C. Jones, Director.
Thos. Magee, Moderator.
John Clopper, Treasurer.
Mattie E. Martin, Teacher.

All Contracts should be made in duplicate, one for the School District and

Teachers Contract —
agreement entered into June 29, 1907 between School
District No. 153 in Gage
County Nebraska and Mattie
Martin, a qualified teacher of said
County. Mattie agreed to keep qualified
as a teacher, and to do her own janitor
work for $35.00 a month — Mattie
Martin later
married Homer F. Morse —
a Morgan County resident.

Teacher — Lura Elkerton (1913)
Adena School (see page 36-40) is shown in
the Background.

IV.

TEACHER CONTRACTS

    A 1920s teacher contract varied by region, but several standards appear to be constant. Contracts for men and women were different. A few of the standard clauses that appeared on woman's contracts were as follows:

> Not to get married, Not to have company with men, to be home between the hours of 8 p.m. and 6 a.m., not to loiter downtown, not to leave town at any time without the permission of the Chairmen of the Trustees, not to smoke cigarettes, not to drink beer, wine, or whiskey, not to dress in bright colors, not to dye her hair, to wear at least two petticoats, not to wear dresses more than 2 inches above the ankles, not to wear face powder, mascara or to paint the lips. Pay was typically $75 per month. (Suki)

A one-room school teacher could not escape essential janitorial and caretaker duties—there simply was no one else to do it. It was necessary to sweep the floor daily with an oil and sawdust compound, routinely dust all the furniture, clean the slate boards, carry out ashes, supply the outhouses with paper, and carry in wood or coal and kindling for the next day. They had to dispose of trash, empty the water bucket and lock all the windows. That done, the teacher could close up and leave the school, carrying the day's papers to grade, and lessons plans for the next day.

V.

EXPERIENCES OF HELEN UNDERWOOD

I taught my first school in 1914 some miles north of Snyder, Colorado for fifty dollars a month.

No school had been established in the community, and I did not begin to teach until January.

The school was held in a one room homestead house. It was heated mostly with corn cobs and some coal. I tacked large sheets of wrapping paper on the walls for blackboards and wrote with crayons.

No books were available so I borrowed some from the Brush School. We carried all our drinking water along with our lunches each day.

People were homesteading the lands. Times were hard, and the people were a hardy lot.

I stayed with a family of five, and three of them were my pupils. The house had one room, and a corner was curtained off for me.

Coyotes howled most of the time. I was twenty miles from home, but it was horse and buggy days. I only went home twice in the five months.

I think often of the children at that make-do school house on the prairie.

From: *History of East Morgan County*

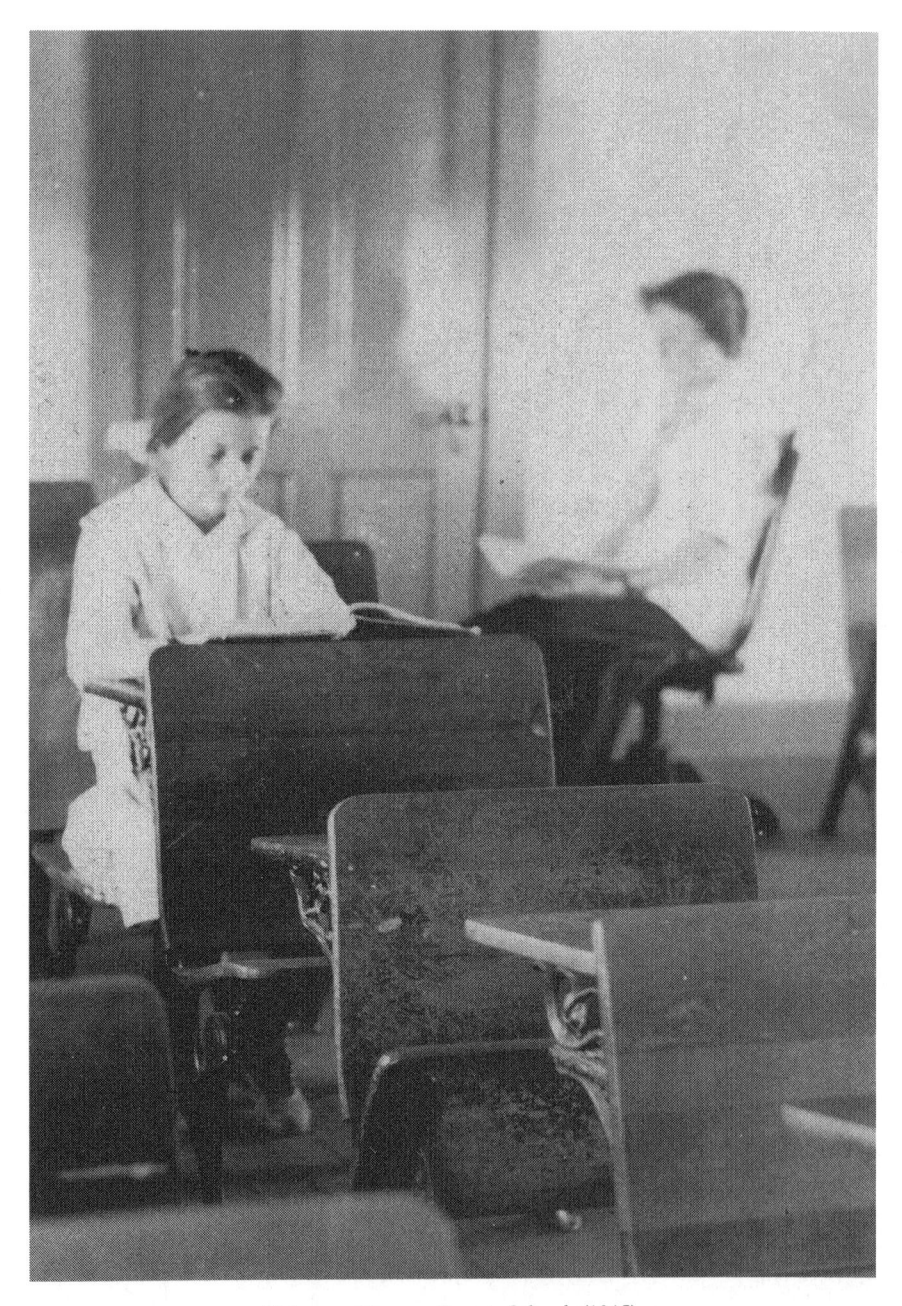

Unknown Morgan County School (1915)
Image courtesy of the Library of Congress

VI.

A DAY IN THE LIFE OF TEACHER AND STUDENT

7:00 a.m.

Arrive at school riding a horse, or by driving a buggy or a car; riding a bike, or walking a mile or two. Next, build a fire in the stove if needed. Pump water from the outside well for drinking and hand washing. Lay out lesson plans and supplies for the day for grades one through eight.

8:00 a.m.

Ring the outside bell.

8:15a.m.

Begin the school day with the Pledge of Allegiance, and in earlier times the Lord's Prayer. Commence learning, with each grade having fifteen minutes up front on a recitation bench. Subjects covered throughout the day were: Reading, Arithmetic, Geography, Spelling, History, Grammar, Penmanship, and on most Fridays, Music and Art. The students worked at their desks, and when needed, older students helped the younger ones with their assignments.

10:00 a.m. to 10:30 a.m.

Recess, inside or outside, depending on the weather.

10:30 a.m.

Lessons resumed, school work in all grades continued until lunch time.

12:00

Lunch and Recess: Many, if not most, of the children's school lunches were carried from home in half-gallon lard buckets. The lunch bucket usually held sandwiches made from home-made bread, butter and jam, fried eggs, head cheese and tongue. On occasion a "Stone Soup" was made in the classroom in a large pot. To make it the children would have brought some sort of vegetable, and the teacher provided soaked beans. The Soup was placed on the stove in the morning and cooked until it was served at noon.

One rather sad, but significant, school lunch story was chronicled in *Capper's Readers*. It tells of a family of six needy children who attended the same school in the years of Great Depression:

> The lunch for these children on a given day might be one small unpeeled potato and two black walnuts. It was explained that the children spent a good deal of time peeling their potato and cracking their two black walnuts on the school's front step in "slow action." so that they would finish eating about the same time as the other students. The story goes on to tell, however, that there were times when other children shared portions of their own lunches with their less-fortunate classmates.

1:00 p.m.

School work resumed, often with twenty minutes or so of reading from a favorite novel – from novels recounting the adventures of *Toby Tyler*, and the heroes and heroines of the *Riders of the Purple Sage* and *Along the Navajo Trail*, and others. The teacher also had to spend extra time during the day with those seventh and eighth graders who would be taking their two-day exam to graduate.

The school day's lessons continued until around **3:45 p.m.**, when students cleaned their desks and got ready to leave, and at **4:00 p.m.** they were dismissed and sent home.

VII.

EXPERIENCES OF
THELMA (KENTOPP) DOWNING

In 1952, I was a teacher in a one-room school in western Nebraska. At the age of eighteen I had no idea of the responsibility I had been handed. I was so young, and thought I could do anything. I attended summer school at McCook Junior College in order to obtain my Type Three Teaching Certificate, so of course I knew how to teach. I signed an eight month contract for $80.00 a month, promised not to marry, vowed to always be attentive to socially correct behavior; mindful of church and the stigma of bars, and of smoking, and vowed not to be seen where it was not proper to be seen. And so, armed with the book: *Course of Study*, that outlined everything needed to be covered in each grade, I began my teaching career. I became the student's primary educator and their music, art, and P.E. Teacher. I was also custodian, disciplinarian, and fortunately, after a time, a trusted teacher and friend.

My school was ten miles south of McCook, Nebraska. It was so isolated, the nearest neighbor was three miles away. In case of an emergency, there was no telephone to call for help (to be honest I never gave it a thought). Many times I walked the mile and a half to school because the snow had drifted the side-road closed. I sometimes think back, wondering what I would have done in a real emergency, with no car and no one close. Fortunately nothing of the sort ever happened.

My first day of school held a few surprises. A student thought my name was "honey" and at 10:30 the students said it was time for their two hour recess, and at noon they expected another hour and a half recess. The teacher before me had given them all of these recesses. I did not see it that way, and so the recess schedule changed that first day. As a result of those long recesses my students were rather behind, and I began the job of catching them up to their respective grade levels. We covered many miles of learning that year and the students jumped two grade levels in their work.

All teachers knew the County Superintendent would pay the class a surprise visit. The thought of that struck terror in my heart. Then one day there was that knock at the door, and it was the Superintendent. As it happened, the day before I had gone over some lessons many times, and as she walked in, we were once-more reviewing these lessons. After her visit she told me she had never heard the students recite so well. Lucky me!

As the school year ended I was told that School Board wanted to rehire me, give me a raise, and said I could even get married. But I said goodbye to my students with tears in my eyes and left to marry, and that ended my amazing experience as a teacher in a one-room school. Many years later I returned to the class-room to teach Art and to serve as School Librarian, but I must here say that I learned more about teaching in my first school than I learned from all the years of courses taken at the University of Northern Colorado.

I often think of the early teachers who taught and endured the many hardships of doing so. Countless of the teachers of yesterday were the brightest and the smartest of women. Their students were blessed. To all of the One-Room School Teachers of long ago: Thank you!

Thelma Downing
Fort Morgan, CO
September, 2016

VIII.

SCHOOL YARD GAMES

    Recess, then, as today was anticipated. Children attending one room schools all played together, grades one to eight were included. Games were designed so all ages and sizes of students could participate. The players had to be self-governing and settled their own disputes. Teachers rarely supervised play; most worked during recess. Pupils in country schools became accustomed to competition and cooperation with various ages. Equipment was scarce — students used sticks, rocks, tin cans, fixed objects such as fences, trees, and the schoolhouse itself in their games. They learned to improvise in the absence of resources.

Baseball at Victory School (c. 1945)

Oxen in Weldon Valley (1905)

Musgrave Homestead (1900)

Many one-room school houses were often built on skids so they could be moved as populations changed. Teams of horses or oxen were often used to move the building.

IX.

MOVING SCHOOL HOUSES

Over 100 school sites in Morgan County are believed to have existed. However, it is difficult to determine exactly how many school houses were constructed as the buildings were often moved. A quote titled: "Funding Sate Education" from the *North Forty News and Fossil Creek Current* reads:

> Researching the Morgan County one-room country schools was found to be somewhat difficult and confusing, because the schoolhouses were, from time to time, moved from place to place, from section to section, from farm to farm, as needed, to more effectively serve the scattered inhabitants of the various communities. It is noted that some of the smaller schools were built on skids to facilitate their moving. Some schools were actually closed, permanently or just for a time, and any left-over children of school age were absorbed by the closest nearby school. The County Map identifies ninety six sites, but, because they were moveable, the actual number of buildings is questionable. It is reported that they were actually moved using two teams of horses and quite likely the relocated school was re-named at its new site. As the population of children moved so did the schools.

An excerpt from the book *Colorado Prairie Trails* documents a school relocation:

> It reports that moving the school was another favorite sport of Morgan County. Whenever enough people in one part of a district decided they wanted the schoolhouse nearer to them the battle was on. Our schoolhouse was named "Fight" because people named Fight had lived next to the school in the early days, but when the neighbors in the south end of the district failed in the vote to get the building moved nearer to them, they promptly began proceedings to divide the district and get a schoolhouse of their own - which they did, and joyously named it "The Victor."

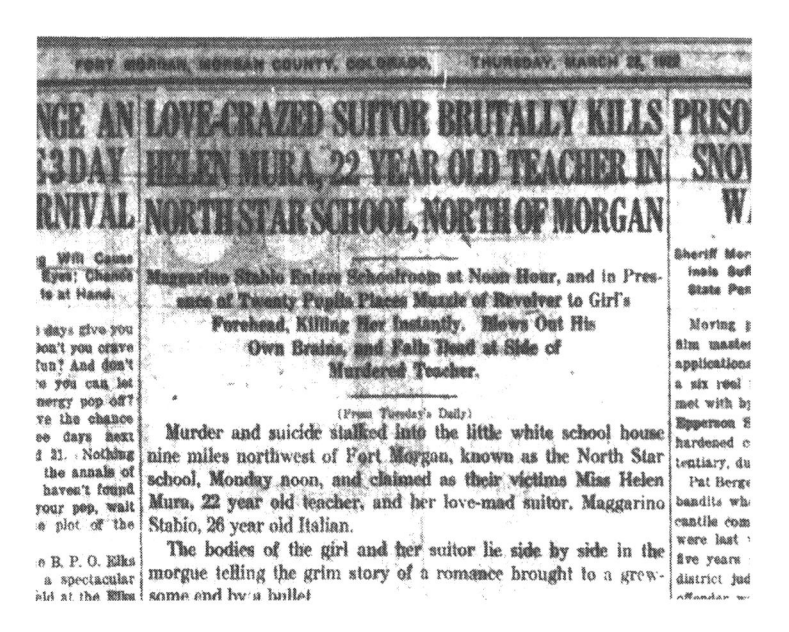

THE ONE ROOM SCHOOLHOUSE: MORGAN COUNTY COLORADO

LOVE-CRAZED SUITOR BRUTALLY KILLS HELEN MURA, 22 YEAR OLD TEACHER IN NORTH STAR SCHOOL, NORTH OF MORGAN

Maggarino Stabio Enters Schoolroom at Noon Hour, and in Presence of Twenty Pupils Places Muzzle of Revolver to Girl's Forehead, Killing Her Instantly. Blows Out His Own Brains, and Falls Dead at Side of Murdered Teacher.

(From Tuesday's Daily)

Murder and suicide stalked into the little white school house nine miles northwest of Fort Morgan, known as the North Star school, Monday noon, and claimed as their victims Miss Helen Mura, 22 year old teacher, and her love-mad suitor, Maggarino Stabio, 26 year old Italian.

The bodies of the girl and her suitor lie side by side in the morgue telling the grim story of a romance brought to a gruesome end by a bullet

Fort Morgan Times — Thursday, March 23, 1922

Helen Mura Gravesite — Riverside Cemetery, Fort Morgan, CO

X.

TRAGEDY AT NORTH STAR SCHOOL

The tragic murder of a young teacher, shot in front of her class, shocked the county. On March 29, 1922, Miss Helen Mura, a twenty two year old teacher, in the one room North Star School, was shot and killed by a "love-mad suitor", Maggarino Stabio, who then shot himself.

Miss Mura was teaching her class of twenty students when Stabio knocked on the outer door of the school. She tried to close the door, but Stabio forced his way in to the small hall where students hung their coats. He spoke in a low and rapid voice. Miss Mura returned to her class and continued teaching. Stabio stayed near the school all morning, even offering a quarter to a little boy if the boy could convince Miss Mura to talk to him.

At noon, he became louder and more insistent. Miss Mura again stepped into the small hall, asking him to leave because he was frightening the children, According to Ben Sailsbury, an older student, Stabio threatened Miss Mura but left. She did not allow the children outside for their usual lunch recess, telling them that she "feared that man outside."

Stabio and Mura had met on her father's farm; Stabio was hired to haul sugar beets. Stabio was immediately smitten by the lovely young woman, but she evidently did not return his interest, at least not at the intensity of his passion.

When school began, Mura moved to the family farm of L.F. Lung, which was close to the school. Stabio moved to Wyoming; he wrote Mura a letter of proposal. It was thought his proposal was rejected. He returned to Colorado, rented an automobile in Weldona, where his behavior seemed nervous to the person who rented him the car. He drove to the North Start School house, dressed in his best clothes.

When J.F. Lung brought her lunch, Mura asked him to bring his wife to the school to stay with her because she was afraid. After Lung left, Stabio again knocked on the outer door; she ignored him, but heard him enter the hall. The twenty children became so frightened that Mura, closing the door, stepped into the hall to plead with him to leave. Instead, Stabio grabbed her, and the children heard scuffling and struggling noises. The door partially opened and the children saw Stabio grab their teacher roughly around the neck, and as she screamed, shot her in the forehead. She died instantly.

He pushed the door open, and, standing in full view of the children, shot himself in the head. Ben Sailsbery reported that the children jumped out of a window so they wouldn't have to walk over the bodies and in the blood. J.F. Lung heard the commotion from his farm and rushed to the school. He found the bodies.

When notified of his daughter's death, Mr. Mura grabbed a shotgun and went to the school. Men tried to prevent him from entering the school, but he forced his way into the hall, almost stumbling over the body of his daughter. He became hysterical and attacked Stabio's body. It took four men to restrain him and lead him outside. When the sheriff and the coroner arrived, they found the school left in the same condition as when the children fled.

XI.

SURVEY OF MORGAN COUNTY SCHOOLS

This section contains information on ninety-five schools that were once located in Morgan County. Today, the Old Trail School (see page 81) located in Wiggins, is the only completely original one room school in Morgan County. After being moved multiple times, the school was relocated to its present location on High Street across from Wiggins Community Park. In 2004, the Wiggins Historical Society was granted a listing for the Old Trail School on the National Register of Historic Places.

Old Trail School (2015)

Fort Morgan, Colo. (1910)

Morgan County is thirty-six miles square and contains 1296 square miles, or 829,440 acres. Fort Morgan, the county seat, is located at the exact geographical center of the county, seventy-eight miles east of Denver. The county has a fine system of irrigation, there being over two hundred and fifty miles of main ditches in operation. These ditches secure their water supply from the South Platte river and the Beaver and Bijou creeks, and furnish water for the irrigation of 250,000 acres of as fine agricultural lands as there are in the world, 75,000 acres of this land being now in actual cultivation. These lands are very level and can be easily irrigated. There are no cradle knolls or hummocks. The land has an average fall toward the east of ten feet and toward the north of eight feet per mile, which causes the water to spread evenly and entirely over the surface and to be conducted over the land without the building of dykes or cuts in the small lateral ditches and with less labor than almost any other locality in the State. The soil is a dark sandy loam of good depth, with clay subsoil, and is especially free from those qualities that cause hardening or baking after being irrigated. Morgan County has an altitude of 4000 feet above sea level and is adapted to the raising of all crops embraced in what is called common or general farming, including fruits of various kinds, and to this date there has not been a single failure attributable to the soil or locality of any variety or class of crops that have been tried.

Fort Morgan Times — 1899

MORGAN COUNTY ONE ROOM SCHOOLS MAP

Locations—Courtesy of Morgan County Commissioners Office for the use of the Morgan County Schools 1884-1965 map.

MORGAN COUNTY ONE ROOM SCHOOLS MAP

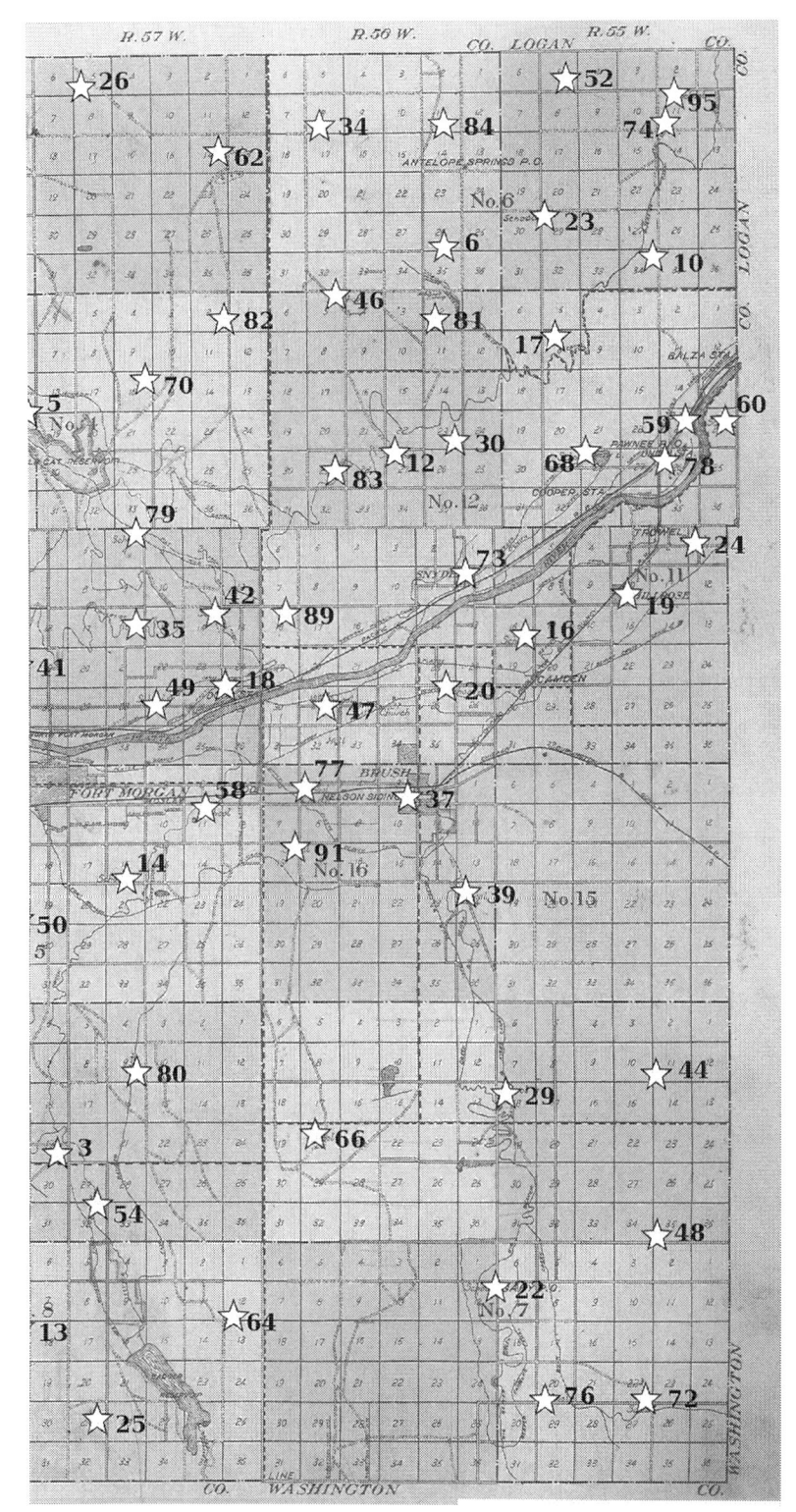

Map: 1913 Atlas

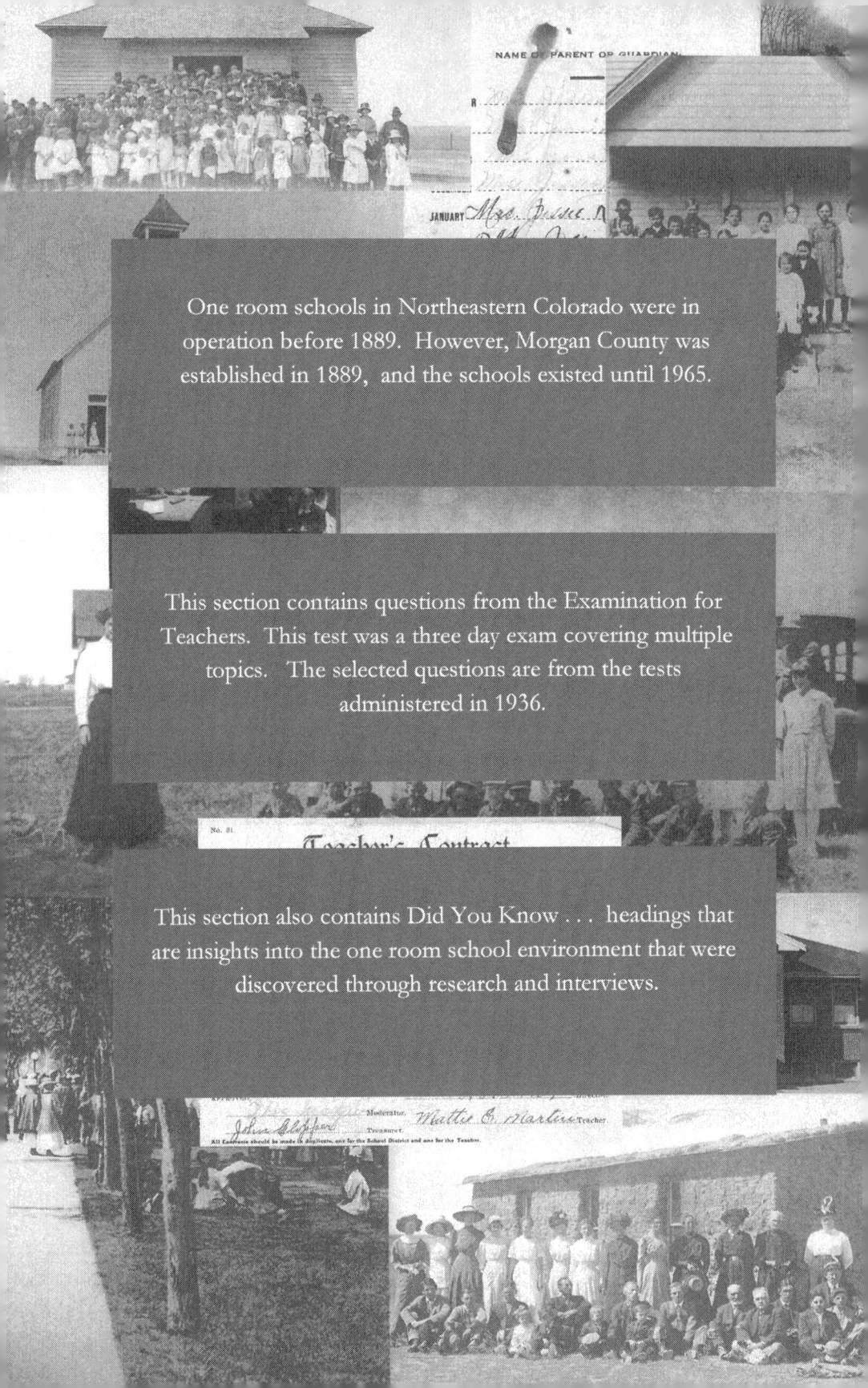

One room schools in Northeastern Colorado were in operation before 1889. However, Morgan County was established in 1889, and the schools existed until 1965.

This section contains questions from the Examination for Teachers. This test was a three day exam covering multiple topics. The selected questions are from the tests administered in 1936.

This section also contains Did You Know . . . headings that are insights into the one room school environment that were discovered through research and interviews.

MORGAN COUNTY ONE ROOM SCHOOLS MAP — KEY

Schools with * asterisk are located on the 1913 Atlas, all school listed can be found on the 1976 Morgan County Commissioners map.

1 Adena
2 Adena*
3 Adena (Newest)
4 Ambrose
5 Antelope Bend
6 Antelope Springs
7 Antelope Valley
8 Beuttler*
9 Bijou View
10 Brammer
11 Bruen
12 Center*
13 Centerville*
14 Chace*
15 Columbine*
16 Colwell
17 Coss
18 Dodd
19 Emerson
20 Fairview*
21 Garfield
22 Gary*
23 Gilliland*
24 Glencoe*
25 Glendale
26 Glenwood
27 Goodrich*
28 Grandview*
29 Hagan*
30 Hayford
31 Hilltop

32 Hopeview*
33 Hoyt*
34 Hunter's Hill
35 Hurley
36 Johnson
37 Knearl*
38 Lake View*
39 Light*
40 Long Meadow*
41 Longs Peak
42 Lower Wildcat*
43 Mac's
44 Midway*
45 Miller
46 Missouri Valley
47 Morey*
48 NE Gary*
49 No. 2*
50 No. 4
51 North Star
52 North Star
53 O'Dell*
54 OK
55 Old Trail
56 Orchard
57 Orchard (1884)
58 Ott*
59 Park*
60 Paul*
61 Peace Valley*
62 Peath*

63 Plainview*
64 Pleasant Ridge
65 Pugh
66 Rauth*
67 Reed*
68 Riverside*
69 Rock Creek*
70 Rock Springs
71 San Arroya
72 SE Gary*
73 Snyder
74 Sunburg
75 Sunnyside
76 SW Gary*
77 Twombly*
78 Union
79 Upper Wildcat*
80 Valley View
81 Valley View*
82 Victory
83 Wandel
84 Welcome Hollow
85 Weldon
86 Weldon Valley
87 West Nile
88 Wiggins
89 Wildcat
90 Willet
91 Williams*
92 Work*
93 Unidentified*
94. Unidentified
95. Unidentified*

MCR = Morgan County Road

1. ADENA

The First Adena School was located in the southwest corner of the intersection of MCRs C and 14, 15 miles south and 4 miles west of Fort Morgan, 2 miles north of the County line. The Adena Post Office was in operation from 1910 to 1947, but a date range for the school has been lost to history. The settlement was named after Edna Adena, who was the sweetheart of an early settler in the area.

Two miles south of this site on MCR 14 at MCR A.3, (three-tenths mile north of the County line), there is a building that is made from the obvious joining of two schoolhouses. It was reportedly used by the Adena Lions Club for some years as a meeting place. It is presently unknown where these two schools originated.

2. ADENA *

The Second Adena School was located 12 miles south and 3½ miles west of Fort Morgan on MCR F at MCR 13.6 on the north side of MCR F. Two foundations are found on the site, one for the school, measuring 20 feet by 40 feet, and one for a teacher's living quarters, measuring 15 feet by 20 feet. The smaller foundation has been filled in with concrete to provide a large stock watering tank. The schoolhouse has been moved to a neighboring farm and made into a garage.

Sample Questions from Teacher Examination —
Physical Geography section— select best answer.

The worlds greatest source of coffee is
(a) Java, (b) Brazil ,(c) the West Indies (d) Mocha.

The most valuable fruit crop in the United States is the
(a) peach, (b) orange, (c) apple, (d) Melon

Answers: B, B

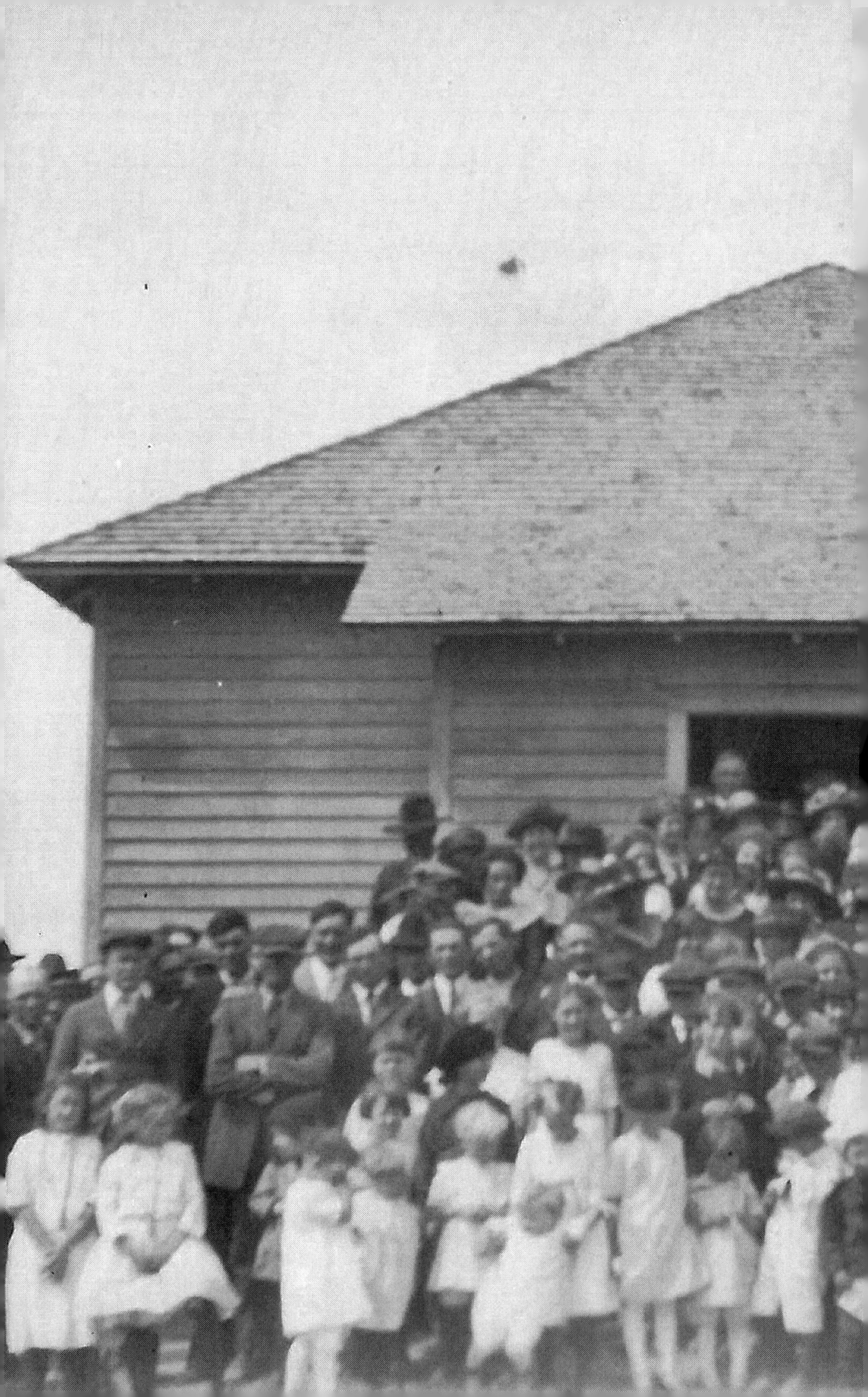

Adena School (c. 1920)

The Adena area was known for their Sunday School and Chapel rallies. Many of the gatherings were organized by residents of nearby Fort Morgan.

3. ADENA (NEWEST)

The third [modern] Adena School was located on MCR I at MCR 18.75, 9 miles due south of Fort Morgan (one of the "Nine Mile Corners" in the County).

Sod Schoolhouse—Adena (1912)

From left to right: Mrs. Edna Hawthorne, Mrs. Hauermann, Mrs. E. H. Groves, Mrs. Neville, Mrs. Fyar in front Mrs. Tompkins and baby Gale, and Mrs. Schneitman.

Did you Know . . .

The teacher's residence, or teacherage, was often attached to the school, or very close by, so that a male teacher's wife and family were an integral part of the management and support system for the school. Single, female teachers were more often billeted or boarded with a local family to provide for social norms requiring social supervision of single females.

4. AMBROSE

Ambrose School (1916)

The Ambrose School was located in the southwest corner of the intersection of MCR P and MCR 14, 2 miles south and 4 miles west of Fort Morgan.

5. ANTELOPE BEND

2015

Did you know . . .

The New England Primer and the 19th Century McGuffey Readers are two of the best-known school books in the history of American education. Of the two, McGuffey's was the most widely used. Over 120 million copies of McGuffey's Readers were sold between 1836 and 1960. The Readers are still in use today in a few school systems, and by parents for home schooling purposes. They continue to sell at a rate of some 30,000 copies per year.

The Antelope Bend School was located on MCR 18 at MCR AA.8 on the west side of MCR 18, 8¾ miles due north of Fort Morgan on Colorado Hwy 52 (MCR 18).

Sample Question from Teacher Examination — History of Colorado Section.

The great cattle kings were gradually forced out of Colorado by
(a) the sheep industry
(b) the establishment of law and order,
(c) the homestead farmers,
(d) the failure of the markets in the east.

The first territorial governor was
(a) Gilpen (b) Evans,
(c) Routt, (d) Tabor

Answers: C, A

6. ANTELOPE SPRINGS

The Antelope Springs School was located in northeast Morgan County on MCR FF at MCR 28.35 on the north side of MCR FF, 8 miles north and ½ to ¾ mile west of Snyder. What appears to be the one acre school site is clearly evident on an aerial photograph of the site. The school building, pictured above, however, was moved to a farmstead approximately one mile north and a half-mile east of the original school site, where it was reinforced, boarded up and used as a granary.

7. ANTELOPE VALLEY

Antelope Valley School (1922)
Anna Busch and nine of her students are sitting on the front steps of the school.
Several of the boys were absent as they had to work in the field that day.

The Antelope Valley School was located on MCR I at MCR 3.4 on the north side of MCR I, 8 miles south and ¾ mile west of Wiggins. The Antelope Valley School was opened in 1912 as one of the five schools built that year for $2,000.

8. BEUTTLER *

The Beuttler School was located in the southwest corner of the intersection of MCR U and MCR 3 at 2091 MCR U, 4 miles north and 1 mile west of Wiggins. The Beuttler School was opened in 1912 as one of the five schools built that year by District 12 for the total sum of $2,000.

Sample Question from Teacher Examination — American Literature section.

The man who wrote a book about his voyage from Boston to California around Cape Horn was
(a) Joseph Lincoln,
(b) Mark Twain,
(c) Irvin S. Cobb,
(d) Richard Dana Jr.

The hero of "O Captain, My Captain" was
(a) Woodrow Wilson,
(b) John Paul Jones,
(c) Abraham Lincoln,
(d) John Smith

Answers: D, C

Did you know . . .

Typically the County Superintendent made a visit to every country school twice a year.

At a noon visit with the pupils, the Superintendent inquired of a girl:

"What do you call your pony?"

The child replied "Mom said to call her Sleepy because she is slow and lazy like you."

(The man blushed.)

9. BIJOU VIEW

Bijou View School was located in southwest Morgan County, in the southwest quadrant of the intersection of the extended lines of MCR G and MCR 10, 10 miles south and 4 miles east of Wiggins. There are noticeable foundation and playground ruins at the site in the northeast corner of Section 3, T1N, R58W. It appears that when it was no longer needed for a school, the building was relocated approximately one mile west and about one-quarter mile north, to its present hilltop site, to be converted into a long-since abandoned farm residence.

Sample Question from Teacher Examination
— Current Events section — True or False?

Greece has recently changed from a monarchy to a republic.

Mexico has recently granted the right to vote to its women citizens.

Answers: T, F

10. BRAMMER

2014

2014

The Brammer School was located in the southwest corner of the intersection of MCR FF and MCR 34, 8 miles north and 5 miles east of Snyder. There is an unbroken 20 foot by 30 foot concrete foundation on this site, in very good condition.

Did you know . . .

Boys liked to make spit wads and flip them to the ceiling or at each other.

(Only when teachers were not looking of course)

To make a wad one chews a piece of paper until juicy, then flip it with the thumb. If it was a good one it would splatter out and stick to the ceiling.

Did you know...

Stone soup was one of the first school hot lunches. Students found a stone, washed it and placed it in a cast iron pot of water on the top of the classroom stove. Vegetables which students brought were added and the soup was that day's hot lunch. The children learned that by those contributing what they brought, a greater good was achieved.

Did the stone make the soup delicious?

11. BRUEN

The Bruen School was located in the northeast corner of the intersection of MCR L and MCR 20, 5 miles south and 2 miles east of Wiggins. In 1912 five schools were built in the southwest part of the County by District 12 for the total sum of $2,000. Bruen was one of them.

12. CENTER *

This mapped school site is located by the Schools Map in the southeast corner of the intersection of MCR AA and MCR 27, 8 miles due north of Brush.

Sample Question from Teacher Examination— Physics Section

The laws of falling bodies were first formulated by
(a) Archimedes,
(b) Galileo,
(c) Boyle,
(d) Pascal

Answer: B

13. CENTERVILLE *

Centerville School (1914)

The Centerville School was located in far southern Morgan County in the southwest corner of MCR 18 at the extended line of MCR E, 14 miles straight south of Fort Morgan.

Sample Question from Teacher Examination —
Geometry section

A line segment connecting two points on a circle is called a ....?

Can the area of a rectangle always be found from its perimeter?

Given a right triangle whose sides are 16 and 12. What is the length of the hypotenuse?

Answers: Chord, Yes, 20

Hazel Ripley's Report Card from Chace School—1913

Monthly report cards were issued and required to be signed by parents. The teacher was Eldora Farr.

14. CHACE *

The Chace School site was located on MCR P at MCR 20.5 on the north side of MCR P, 2 miles south and 1½ miles east of Fort Morgan.

15. COLUMBINE *

The school is mapped as the "Columbine" school. However, the school is correctly known as the "Pleasant Prairie School." Columbine was the name of the little community in northwest Morgan County which was served by the Pleasant Prairie School. The Pleasant Prairie School District No. 14 was organized on September 3, 1911. It was located on MCR HH at MCR 2.86 on the north side of MCR HH, 9 miles north and 2½ miles west of Goodrich. In 1965 the Pleasant Prairie School was closed when District 14 was dissolved; Pleasant Prairie students were schooled in Weldona.

16. COLWELL

The map location for the Colwell School in eastern Morgan County, is the northwest corner of the intersection of MCR V and MCR 31, 1 mile south and 2 miles east of Snyder. Following consolidation of the rural schools, the Colwell School building, like Fairview, its "sister" school, was converted into a nice home, and it served as such until it burned. The following information was taken from a paper supplied by Mrs. Alice Colwell that appears in the *History of East Morgan County:*

Colwell School (1940)
Image courtesy of Betty Baker

> ... The Colwell School was built in 1890 and was named the Colwell School in deference to the help of C.I. Colwell in establishing the school. It measured 22 feet by 30 feet and was painted white. There were 8 or 10 pupils that first year and first teacher was Miss L. Plowhead ... After some eight years, the original school became too small and was moved to the Henry Lauck farm adjoining the original school site on the west, and a new, larger school was built in 1899 on the site of the original school. It had two outside entries, a library was between. The School had a belfry with a bell. The bell rope hung down into the small library room ... In 1922 a new, much larger room was added on the east side of the building which was later divided into two good sized rooms by adding folding doors in the middle of the room to make three separate rooms for three teachers, teaching all grades up to and including the first year of High School first taught in 1923. The doors were folded back to allow the larger space to be used for an auditorium for programs, PTA meetings and various social functions ... Kerosene lamps in brackets were used to light the rooms for evening gatherings. A few years later Colman gasoline lanterns were loaned by different families to help with the lighting.

17. COSS

The Coss School was located on the south side of MCR DD at MCR 31.45. The first Coss School was held in a dugout. In 1919 a new school was built and it was withdrawn from Snyder Dist. No. 1, forming district No. 16. In 1937, the children from Coss were transported by bus to Gilliland or Riverside schools. An aerial photo shows ruins that have the appearance of a collapsed building that are the approximate size of a school building.

18. DODD

Dodd School was located in the northeast corner of the intersection of MCR 23 and MCR T.9, 2½ miles north and 4 miles east of Fort Morgan. A railroad and a post office was located about eight or nine miles northeast of Fort Morgan on the Union Pacific Railroad, The Dodd Post Office was in operation from 1904-1907 (Shaffer 253).

19. EMERSON

The Emerson School site is located on the map in the Town of Hillrose. The school was first established in 1898 on the Emerson Ranch just east of town near a lake where buffalo wallowed and later the Emerson Ranch horses pastured. In 1889, Jennie Parson taught in the little school in the pasture. Following an election to do so, the school was moved to the present site of the school in the Town of Hillrose in 1901. In 1907 or 1908 a two room-room cement school building was erected and the one-room school was moved down to Main Street and became a real estate office and later a grocery store. In 1915, a brick addition was added to the 1907 school. In 1920 a special election approved the consolidation of the District No. 10, Glencoe, with District No. 5, Hillrose. In 1934, a combination brick gymnasium and auditorium and stage, along with two additional classrooms and a kitchen was added to the school building.

20. FAIRVIEW *

Fairview School was located in eastern Morgan County on MCR U at MCR 28.7 on the south side of MCR U, just 2 miles north and ¾ miles east of Brush. The Fairview School was built in 1888, and was part of Weld County School District No. 96. In 1889 when Morgan County was formed, the School District was designated Morgan County District No. 1, but later lost its standing due to a lack of students. District No. 1 was then merged with Morgan County School District No. 6. In 1900 District No. 6 was reorganized with two schools – Fairview and Colwell, with 122 pupils in both schools. A new one-room Fairview school was built in 1889 to teach all eight grades. A few years later, a second room was added to Fairview school and two teachers were hired. The reorganization and consolidation of the County's rural schools brought about the closing of Fairview and Colwell, its "sister" school, and they were sold and repurposed into homes.

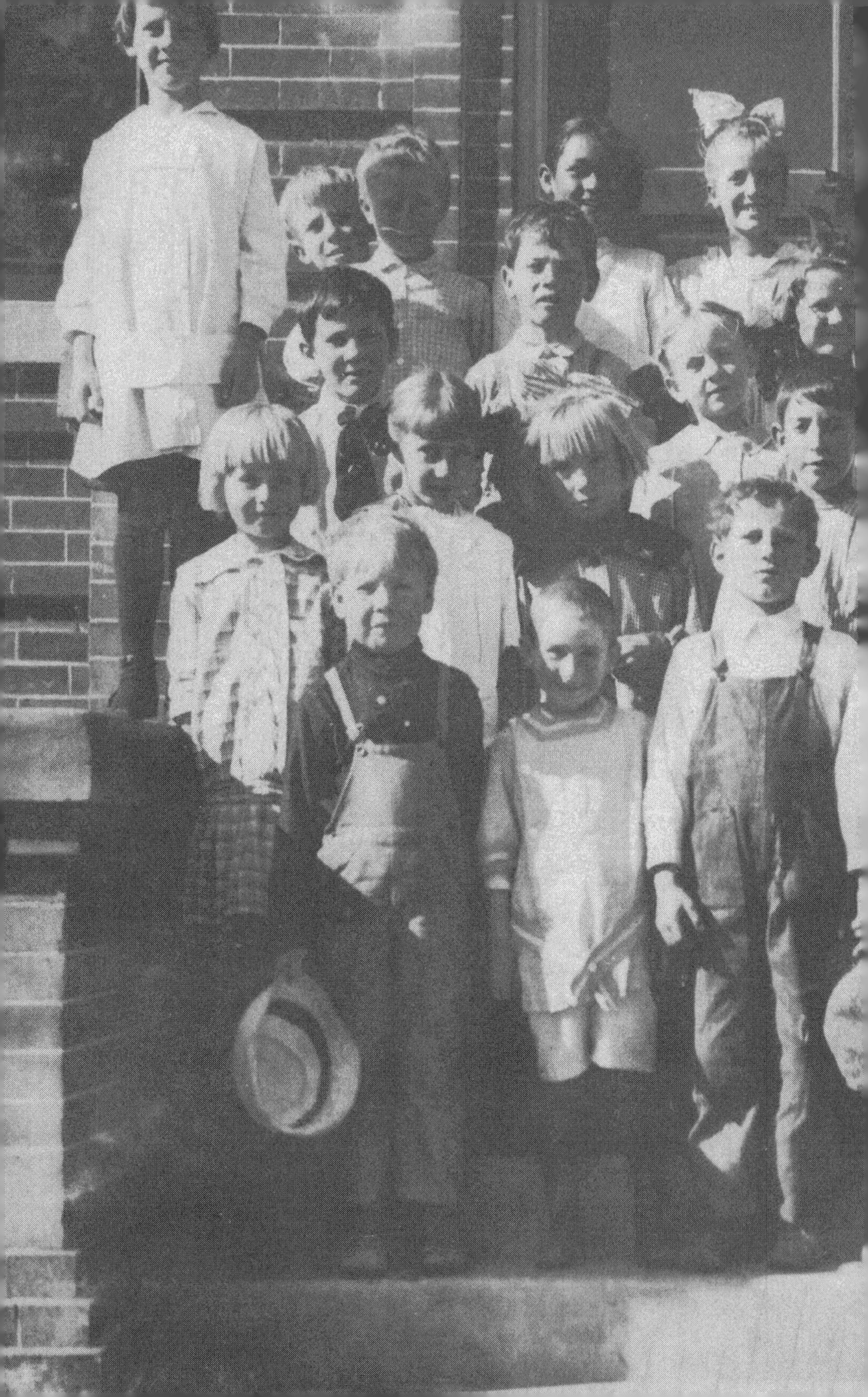

Grant School—Fort Morgan (1915)
Image courtesy of the Library of Congress

21. GARFIELD

Garfield School (1915)

The Garfield School was located by the Schools Map on MCR EE at MCR 0.4 on the North side of MCR EE, 7 miles north of Orchard and approximately four-tenths mile east of the Morgan-Weld County Line.

22. GARY *

In 1890 a group of citizens were gathered to make provisions for a school District, later known as Gary District No. 7, and the first school term at Gary School was held that year in a vacant sod house owned by Thomas Tennant. It was located in southeast Morgan County, three miles south and a quarter mile east of where the Gary Post Office was later established. It is known from research that in 1892 Ella Walks taught a one month school term from June 1st to July 31st with eleven students attending.

In 1893 heating problems for the school were solved by adopting a four month term beginning on March 1st. A six month term was later adopted and constituted the school year for thirty years, until 1923, when a standard nine month term was adopted. In 1898 a 28 foot by 48 foot frame building, reportedly a "dance hall" which included a cloak room, was moved from Abbott Colorado to a location across from the Gary Post Office and became the one-room Gary School. The original sod building was sold for $25.

Although, as time passed, there were four Gary District school locations, the largest number of students resided at Gary proper. All eight grades were taught at the Gary School with "school" beginning at nine o'clock in the morning and ending at four in the afternoon. The school grounds covered about two acres and since many of the students rode horses to school, there was a red barn for the horses. Necessarily, there were two outhouses and a coal shed. The one room school was fairly large with a cloak room at the entrance to store coats, caps, "over boots" when they were worn, and lunch pails, which were often five pound lard buckets that Mom had gotten at the grocery store.

In 1917 a new frame building was built to replace the 1898 "dance hall" school. The last Gary School that served the District is located on MCR 30 at MCR E.8, 12 miles south and 2 miles east of Brush. In 1953 consolidation of the four Gary Schools was approved, and steps were taken for construction of a new building at Gary. The new building was completed in 1955, and the other four buildings were sold. The new Gary school was a brick structure with four classrooms with two grades in each room and a well-equipped kitchen for serving hot lunches. In 1965, in response to measures to equalize Colorado school taxes, the Morgan County School Districts were reorganized, and Gary District No. 7 became part of School District RE-2, Brush. As a result, the Gary seventh and eighth grade students were taken to Brush by bus. Then, in the fall of 1969, all Gary school children were bussed to school in Brush and the Gary School closed.

23. GILLILAND *

Gilliland school was located in the far northeast corner of Morgan County, at the southeast corner of the inter-section of MCR GG and MCR 31, 8 miles north and 2 miles east of Snyder. School for that community's children was first held in homestead shacks that had been "proved-up-on" or in abandoned shacks. The members of the community, however, became determined to find a place large enough to properly accommodate and educate the students. As a result, the Gilliland schoolhouse or Prairie Glen as it was sometimes called was built in 1914-1915. This was the first schoolhouse to be built in northeastern Morgan County. Children came from all around, often-times walking four or five miles. Sam Gilliland, the namesake, was the first teacher. In 1917, an effort was made to consolidate the Gilliland's School District with the Snyder District but the proposition was defeated. In 1937, Gilliland and Riverside took in the children from the Coss and North Star Schools. They were transported to Gilliland by bus.

The school building, as pictured, has been moved from its original location to the south and west at the intersection of MCR EE and the line of MCR 31, where it has been reinforced with cables and converted into a large granary.

24. GLENCOE *

The map location for the Glencoe School is in the northwest corner of the intersection of MCR X at MCR 33.5, 1 mile north and 1 mile east of Hillrose.

25. GLENDALE

The Glendale School was located on the west side of MCR 20 at MCR B.5, 15½ miles south and 1 mile east of Fort Morgan.

Sample Questions from Teacher Examination — Chemistry section.

At what temperature on the Centigrade scale does water boil at sea level?

The chemical name for marble is ....

The nonmetallic element used in vulcanizing rubber is ....

Answers: 100°, calcite or dolomite, sulfur

Did you know . . .

Grades were reported for all subjects taken as well as for "Industrial Work" and "Deportment." As for Deportment there were some instant bad-behavior consequences, like:

* Use of a wood paddle or a switch standing at blackboard with a nose in circle for an hour.

* No recess or a stay after school.

* Sitting in a "Dunce Chair" Parents graded "Industrial Work" by grading home chores.

26. GLENWOOD

The Glenwood School was originally located just one mile south of the County Line in the far north part of central Morgan County, in the northeast corner of the intersection of MCR JJ and MCR 19, 17 miles north and 1 mile east of Fort Morgan. Wes Johnson, a lifetime local resident, when interviewed, reported that the Glenwood School has been moved twice. The first time to a location east and a little south of the original school site and placed, for a time, on the south side of MCR II. The second time it moved 1½ miles farther east and about another ½ mile south to become the principal part of the pictured ranch house. Mr. Johnson explained that the ranch house actually unites two schoolhouses, explaining that a second, smaller, school house - the gabled structure on the left - was moved from a location north of Snyder and incorporated into the home. He was unable to identify the smaller school building.

27. GOODRICH *

The Goodrich School was located at 4280 Hwy. 144, approximately three-quarters of a mile northeast of the town of Goodrich. The School was named after G.W. Goodrich who had built the first and finest home in the valley. The first school was accidently burned down by the Union Pacific Railroad company. The next school was named after Walter Southward, and was built in 1892 behind the site that burned. In 1908, a new building was constructed. An addition to the school was built in 1912.

> Sample Question from
> Teacher Examination
> — English Literature
>
> Chaucer's greatest and most
> original piece of work
> was written in
> (a) French,
> (b) English,
> (c) Latin,
> (d) Italian
>
> Answer: B

Did you know . . .

Teachers that taught in the one room, rural schools always took care of their students.

During winter months, they would arrive at the school early to get a fire started in the potbelly stove.

On many occasions, they would prepare a hot meal on top of the stove consisting of soup or stew of some kind.

The County School at Goodrich (c. 1910)
The photograph's back reads: "... located just east of where the Goodrich road curves to intersect with Jackson Lake Road (picture view to the north)." Above the doorway, a sign reads "1881 Goodrich No. 8 District."

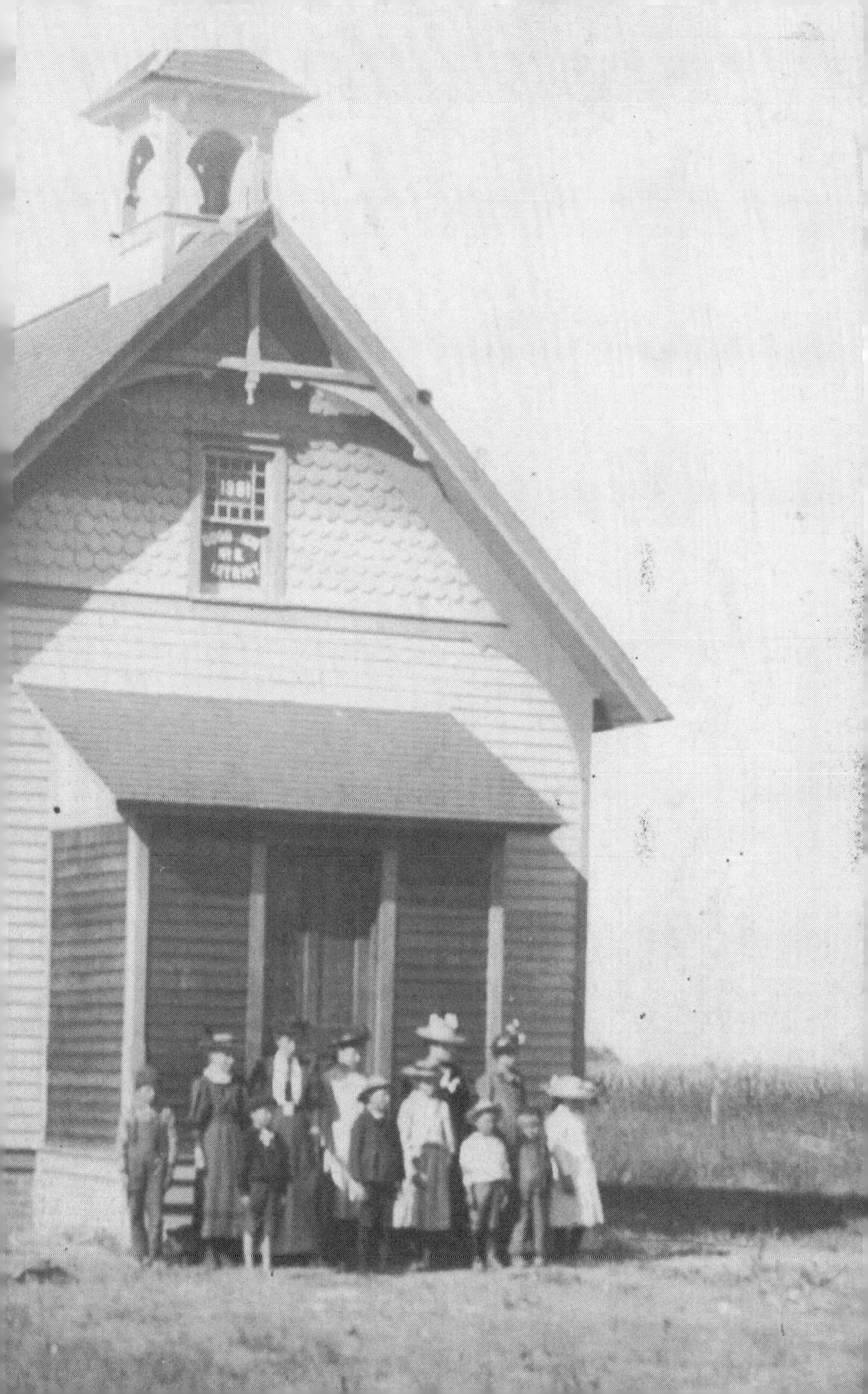

28. GRANDVIEW *

Grandview School was located on MCR 17 at MCR W.5 on the west side of MCR 17, 4½ miles north and 1 miles west of Fort Morgan.

29. HAGAN *

The Hagan School was located on MCR 30 at MCR J.5 on the east side of MCR 30, 7¼ miles south and 2 miles east of Brush. The land for the school was donated to Brush School District No. 2, now known as RE-2 in 1902 by a Mr. Hagan, the landowner, and the school was named Hagan School. Mamie Wetzbarger from a paper submitted to History of East Morgan County tell us:

> ... the school is in "that small group of trees south of the Nine Mile Corner across the road from the Jim Hunt Farm." ... Miss Searles, the teacher in 1902, is remembered as a stylish lady, decked out with her hoops and bustle, loping across the prairie riding side-saddle on a brown horse at a slow lope. This lady (Searles—Anderson) later became Morgan County Superintendent of Schools. She drove a team of matched blacks to work in Ft. Morgan. The Hagan School is remembered as a one-room building with a small entry at the front where coats were hung and overshoes were stacked. There was a pump in the school yard for the water supply. Two outdoor toilets were way back to the east end of the school yard, one on the north corner for the boys and one on the south corner for the girls with a barn in between for the horses of those kids who rode to school.

30. HAYFORD

The Hayford School was located at MCR 28.6 on MCR AA on the north Side of MCR AA, 3 miles north and ¼ mile west of Snyder, just off CO Hwy 71.

31. HILLTOP

The Hilltop School was located on the west side of MCR 15 at MCR H.8, 9 ½ miles south and 3 miles west of Fort Morgan.

32. HOPEVIEW *

The Hopeview School was located on MCR 14 at MCR II.7 on the East side of MCR 14, 16½ miles north and 4 miles west of Fort Morgan. Hopeview was built in 1911 at the same time that Peace Valley (see pg. 88) was built. In 1926, the students and faculty at Hopeview and the Peace Valley School were consolidated at Peace Valley.

Did you know . . .

In early days slate tablets and chalk were used. Later the supplies were pencils, Big Chief Tablets and Crayons, and in the fourth grade a pen, pen points, and ink were on the list.

Many braids were dipped in the ink wells.

33. HOYT *

*Listed on the State Register *   2014

The Hoyt School is located in the far southwest corner of Morgan County at 3500 MCR B, approximately one-half mile west of the intersection of MCR B with MCR 4, 15 miles south and ½ mile west of Wiggins and 1 mile north of the Morgan County line. The Hoyt School was built in 1918, and served as the education center for the community from the time of its construction until consolidation forced closure in 1946. The grounds and outbuildings of the school now function as the Hoyt Community Center. The Hoyt School and Community Building is listed in the Colorado State Register of Historic Buildings.

The first Hoyt School was established in 1888 as part of Weld County School District No. 95, and was a dugout in the bank of Bijou Creek. It was operated primarily by donation, although there was a small amount of state aid for a teacher's salary. When Morgan County was created in 1889, the Hoyt School was immediately transferred to Morgan County's School District No. 5.

During the Great Depression in the mid to late 1930's, the Works Progress Administration (WPA), constructed an addition to the south and west sides, which included a stage at the head of the classroom and stairs leading to a basement.

> The W.P.A. didn't construct many rural schools; however, basement excavations designed to add more usable space for students were typical projects of this New Deal era federal relief program. The basement excavation at the Hoyt School was completed by the WPA and included a small kitchen where hot lunches were made for students. The adjoining larger room served as a cafeteria where students could eat what might possibly be their only complete and hot meal of the day.
>
> (Baughn)

34. HUNTER'S HILL

The Hunter's Hill School was located on MCR II at MCR 25.4 on the north side of MCR II, 16 miles north and 1½ miles west of Brush.

35. HURLEY

The Hurley School was located on MCR 20.5 at MCR V.3 on the east side of MCR 20.5, 3½ miles north and 2½ miles east of Fort Morgan.

36. JOHNSON

The Johnson School was located at 00010 MCR N V, 3 miles south and app. 3½ miles West of Wiggins, just east of the Morgan-Weld County Line.

37. KNEARL *
(see photograph page 70-71)

The Knearl School is located on MCR 28 at Rd, Q.3, a.k.a. 314 Clayton Street, within the Brush Municipal Park. Knearl School was built in 1910 south of the railway. The school was named for William Knearl, who once served as School Board President of the Brush area School District No. 2, and who donated land for the school. When Knearl opened it served the educational needs of children in grades one through eight, but at the time of its closing in the Spring of 1971, it was serving only first, second, and third graders. When no longer needed for a school, the building was acquired by the Town of Brush and serves as its municipal museum.

Did you know . . .

With the influx of immigrant homesteaders, Danish and German-Russian, to the Brush community, new rural schools were built. Six such schools were established by the Brush school board: Hagan, Light, Liberty, Twombly, Williams and Smith Schools.

From:
History of East Morgan County

Sample Question from
Teacher Examination
—— Arithmetic section

25% of 24 is ....

A .... is a figure with three sides

Answers: 6, Triangle

38. LAKE VIEW *

The Lakeview school site is located in the northwest corner of the intersection of MCR U and MCR 13, 2 miles north and 5 miles west of Fort Morgan.

39. LIGHT *

Light School (1909) — Image courtesy of Trish Turner

The Map location for the Light School is not far from Brush, in the northeast corner of the intersection of MCR O.5 and MCR 29, 2½ miles south and 1 mile east of Brush. The Light school was a very small one-room school built in 1902 on the Charles Light property south-east of Brush. It was the smallest School in Brush School District No. 2. From separate writings of Katherine George and Alice Colwell — *History of East Morgan County,* we know that pioneer teachers were Mrs. J.M. Hurley, 1906, Helen Rose, Efay Gregg (Nelson) and Alice Bleasdale in 1911. Miss Bleasdales salary started at $42.50. The $2.50 was for janitorial duties. Teachers did all of the cleaning and saw to the heating of the building. The Light School was closed in 1916; the students were bussed to Brush.

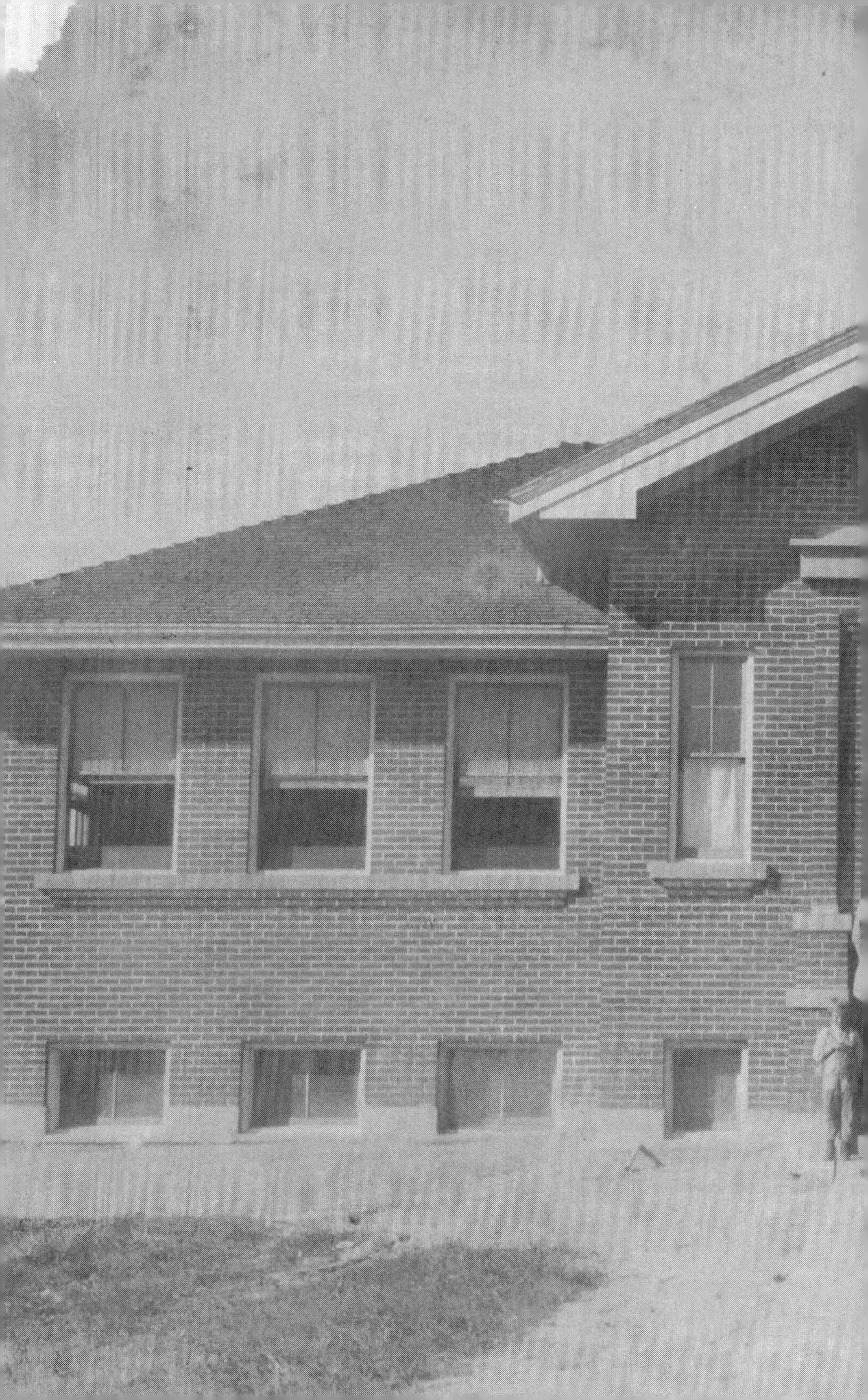

Knearl School (1915) — Courtesy of the Library of Congress

40. LONG MEADOW *

Listed on the State Register 2014

   The Long Meadow School is located in the southwest part of Morgan County in the northeast corner of the intersection of MCR I and MCR6, at 60000 MCR I, 8 miles south and 2 miles east of Wiggins. Long Meadow School was opened in 1908. As originally constructed, the 1908 schoolhouse consisted of a rectangular plan with an entry door centered in the south elevation. The exterior walls were clad in horizontal wood siding and the roofing consisted of cut wood shingles. Early photos show that the south gable end once contained a return cornice. The school building measured 16 feet east to west by 26 feet north to south. In 1933 a 10 foot by 12 foot cloakroom was added to extend the south entrance.

   In 1949 one half of a former army barracks was moved to the site from Buckley Field in Aurora, Colorado and joined to the west side of the building, and the combined structure became, the Long Meadow Community Club Building. The School and the Long Meadow Club Building are listed in the State Register of Historic Buildings.

41. LONGS PEAK

Longs Peak School was located on MCR 18 (CO Hwy 52) between MCR U and MCR V on the west side of MCR 18, 2½ miles due north of Fort Morgan.

42. LOWER WILDCAT

The Lower Wildcat School was located in the southeast corner of the intersection of MCR W and MCR 23, 4 miles north and 4 miles east of Fort Morgan.

Sample Question from Teacher Examination — Sanitation and Hygiene Section— True or False?

The white blood corpuscles are the body's scavengers.

Fats are digested in the small intestine.

There are no blood vessels in bone tissues

Answers: T, T, F

Did you know . . .

The most common medicine was castor oil and after one dose, no one asked for more.

Kerosene was used for wasp and bee stings, for insect bites, and for frostbite.

What pleasant smells in the school house?

43. MAC'S

MAC's School was located on MCR X at MCR 14.3 on the south side of MCR X, 5 miles north and 3 miles west of Fort Morgan.

44. MIDWAY *

The Midway School was located in the northwest corner of the Intersection of MCR K and MCR 34, 7 miles south and 6 miles east of Brush, just 2 miles west of the Washington County line.

45. MILLER

The Miller School was located in the northeast corner of the intersection of MCR O and MCR 6, 2 miles south and two miles east of Wiggins. The Miller School was opened as one of the five schools built that year in the southwest part of the County by District No. 12 for the total sum of $2,000.

46. MISSOURI VALLEY

The Missouri Valley School was located in the southwest corner of the intersection of MCR EE and MCR 26, 12 miles north and 1 mile west of Brush.

Sample Question from Teacher Examination — History of the United States section — true or false?

The three types of government in the early colonies were charter, royal and proprietary.

The fist political parties started during Madison's term as President

Answers: T, F.

47. MOREY *

The Morey School site is just northwest of Brush in the northwest corner of the intersection of MCR T.5 and MCR 26. It is approximately 2 miles west and 2 miles north of Brush upon land donated by A. J. Morey. Originally, it was a one-room frame building where children in grades one through eight were taught by one teacher. In 1914 a new brick school was built at that same location and served until 1933. Two large classrooms were separated by a wide hallway where there space was provided for the children's wraps and for storage of their lunch baskets. There was a library on one side of the front doorway and a wash room on the other side. In 1933, a fire destroyed all but the brick walls. A re-built and even more convenient new school was finished in 1934 using the salvaged bricks. This "new" school served the community's needs until the state ordered the reorganization of the District in 1959. It is now a private home.

48. N.E. GARY *

The N.E. Gary School was located in the far southeast corner of Morgan County. It was built to serve the northeast quadrant of the Gary School District at the northeast corner of the intersection of MCR G and MCR 34, in the SW Corner of Section 35. The location of the school was 11 miles south and 6 miles east of Brush and one mile north and four miles east of Gary. In 1913, N.E. Gary School, was opened and functioned as an elementary school, and according to Helen Thornsby, it was always attended by pupils in the elementary grades. When the Gary District was consolidated in 1953, the N.E. Gary School was sold for $340. Remnants of the foundation and other improvements can still be found on its original site. The school building, itself, was moved to a hilltop location a half-mile, or a little more, east and north of its original location, made into a home, and, though now in a semi-ruined state, it is still standing and remains a real image of the original schoolhouse.

49. NO. 2 *

No. 2 School was located on MCR T.5 at MCR 21 (line) on the north side of MCR T.5, 1½ miles north and 2 east of Fort Morgan.

50. NO. 4

School No. 4 was located in the northwest corner of the intersection of MCR O at MCR 18, 3 miles due south of Fort Morgan.

Sample Question from Teacher Examination
— Writing section

The handwriting of pupils does not seem to improve greatly after the
(a) fourth grade,
(b) sixth grade,
(c) ninth grade.

The most important factor in good handwriting is
(a) beauty,
(b) speed,
(c) legibility.

Answers: A, C

Did you know...

During World War II the schools contributed to many war-time projects.

Milkweed pods were picked and gathered at schools. The fluffy insides of the pods were used to make life jackets.

Other school projects were: Gathering tin cans, tin foil and scrap iron.

"Victory Gardens" were planted to raise food.

51. NORTH STAR

North Star School was established in 1916 in the far northeast corner of the County on MCR JJ at MCR 31.6 on the north side of MCR JJ, 17 miles north and 3½ miles east of Brush.

North Star School (1916)
Teacher was Ruth Davis

Mr. Ed Peterson donated the land in 1910, and men from the community built the school in 1911. The school was named "North Star" by Mr. James and Mrs. Whittington in memory of the school they had attended in Iowa. By 1937 the population of the community had declined to the extent that it was no longer feasible to keep the North Star School open, so the area's students were transported by bus to Gilliland.

52. NORTH STAR

School Picnic for North Star School (c. 1920)

A second North Star School was located in the southeast corner of the intersection of MCR 14 and MCR AA (line), 8 miles north and 4 west of Fort Morgan.

53. O'DELL *

The O'Dell School is located in western Morgan County nearly midway between Fort Morgan and Wiggins on the east side of MCR 11 a little south of its intersection with MCR Q, 6½ miles due east of Wiggins.

Sample Question from
Teacher Examination
— History of the Reading section.

The time for a child to begin to read should generally be determined by
(a) the mental age,
(b) the chronological age,
(c) the course of study.

A reading course should consist
(a) mostly of interesting stories,
(b) of informative materials that will help the children to increase their knowledge,
(c) a wide variety of reading materials.

Answers: A, C

Did you know...

A course of study book was given to teachers, which by many was considered a lifeline to sanity. The book was issued by the State of Colorado.

The book provided instruction for teaching all subjects — grades 1 to 8.

54. OK

OK School Students (c. 1945)
Back Row: Donald Tormohlen, Forrest Carver, Larry O'Leary, Darrel Geyer, Richard May, George Glenn, Jewel Meyers, Patty Schreiner, Kathryn 'Kay" Glenn, and Beulah Meyers.
Front Row: Lawrence Tormohlen, Jerry Meyers, Brian Carver, Dean Nichols, Jack Meyers, Floyd Nichols, John Glenn, Virginia Schreiner, Colleen O'Leary, Annette Carver, Lila Geyer, Ila Mae Meyers, and Albert Meyers.
Image courtesy of the Glenn Family Collection

The O.K. School was located in the southwest corner of the intersection of MCRs H (line) and MCR 20, 10 miles south and 1 mile east of Fort Morgan.

55. OLD TRAIL

The Old Trail School was once located on the east side of MCR 6 at MCR E.5, at 54000 MCR 6, which is 11½ miles south and 2 miles east of Wiggins. However, the building now sits in the Town of Wiggins. The school was originally known as the Reed School which was built in 1909 on the George Reed Homestead. The Reed School was located at MCR 3.4 on MCR G at 3400 MCR G on the north side of MCR G, which is 10 miles south and ½ mile west of Wiggins. It was moved from the original site in 1919 to its second location and there re-named "Old Trail School." The name reflects the fact that the school, when moved, was located on the cut-off branch of the "Overland Trail." It was again moved, this time to Wiggins, where it was set on school property and used as a music room. In 1964, it was acquired by the Wiggins Historical Group, and finally moved to its present location at 421 High Street. It is registered with the State and National Register of Historic Places that feature the school as exhibiting the distinguishing characteristics of a typical rural one room school house.

56. ORCHARD

Did you know . . .

The prairie lacked standard building materials such as wood or stone.

The sod schoolhouse was made from thickly-rooted prairie grass. This grass has a much thicker and stronger root structure than modern landscaping grass.

Adena Sod School Interior (1912)

When the Orchard Sod School closed, four wooden school buildings were placed in various locations in the District. The original school in the Town of Orchard, pictured above, sat just west of the water tank. When it was replaced it was moved one block south from that location to the corner of Third Street and Washington Avenue and converted into a private residence.

Sample Question from Teacher Examination — Elementary Science and Agriculture section.

Corn and .... are the two most valuable crops of the United States.

Answer: Wheat

57. ORCHARD (SOD—1884)

Willing Women's Aid Society of Orchard and Goodrich (c. 1890)
This photograph was taken after a minster spoke at the schoolhouse.
The arrow points to Mrs. Hippolyte Giradot of Orchard.

As related in the book *A View of Orchard: Roots and All:*

> ... the first Orchard school was made of sod. It was constructed in 1884 and located on the B. B. Putnam Ranch a half-mile from Orchard. The school was part of Weld School District No. 7. The Sod school closed in 1890.

Sample Question from Teacher Examination
— Spelling section — true or false?

Correct pronunciation should be emphasized as an aid to good spelling.
The poor speller is likely to have a poor method for studying spelling.

Answers: T, T

Orchard School House (c. 1895)
The Teacher was Ada Putman

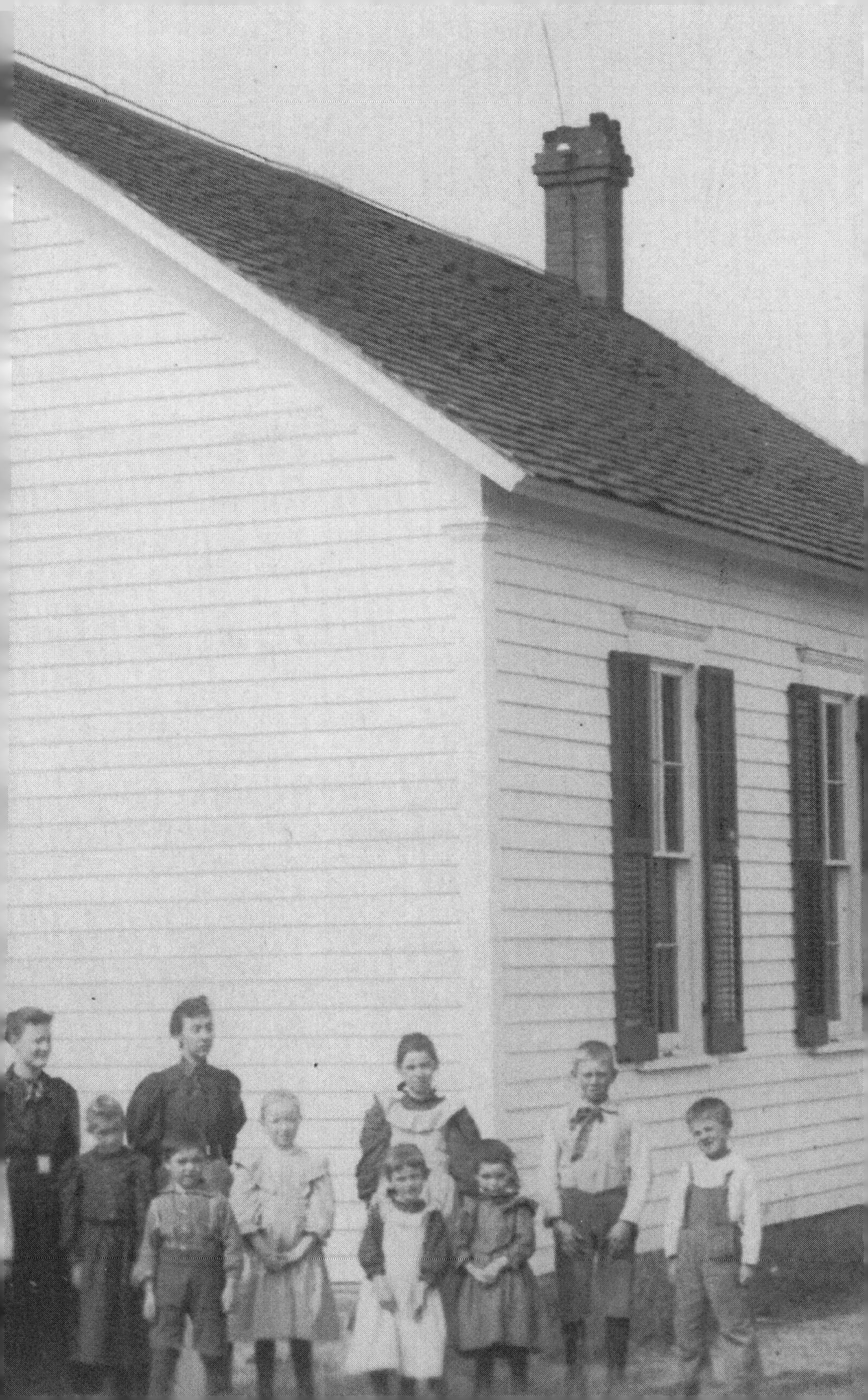

Did you know . . .

Many of the students were very poor immigrants and had little understanding of the English language.

They seldom had proper clothing and shoes.

A typical lunch bucket contained:

Fried eggs and bread

Jelly & Peanut Butter

Homemade hog sausage

Head Cheese
(made from a hogs head, feet, and tongue)

Potatoes, leftovers or anything available.

58. OTT *

The Ott School site was located by the Morgan County Map in the southeast corner of the intersection of MCR R and MCR 22, 3 miles due east of Fort Morgan on Road R. However, it has been discovered, that the Ott School site was located ½ mile east of the previously stated location in the southeast corner of the intersection of MCR R and MCR 22.5 (line).

59. PARK *

Park School was located on MCR W.7 at MCR AA.6 on the southeast side of W.7 near the geographical center of section 23, approximately 4½ miles north and 1½ miles east of Hillrose.

Sample Question from
Teacher Examination
— School Law section —
true or false?

No person shall teach in the public schools of the state unless such person holds a legal certificate pertaining to the schools or classes under his charge.

Answer: T

60. PAUL *

The Paul School was located on the west side of MCR 36 at MCR AA.6 on the Morgan County Line 4½ miles north and 3 miles east of Hillrose. The school was built in 1900 in the southeast corner of the "55 Ranch" across the road from a family by the name of Paul. At the time the "55 Ranch" consisted of all of sections 12, 13, 14 and 24 in Range 55, Township 5 North. The school was located on the far-east side of Section 24.

>Sample Question from Teacher Examination
> — Civics section — true or false?
>
>The Bill of Rights in the Constitution in guaranteeing certain rights to citizens of the United States, places limitations upon the federal government.
>
>The Constitution gives the president the power to declare war.
>
>Answers: T, F

61. PEACE VALLEY *

The Peace Valley School is located 16 miles north and 2 miles west of Fort Morgan on the south side of MCR II at MCR 16.5. The schoolhouse was built by homesteaders in 1911 and, as of this writing, what remains of it, along with familiar items of playground equipment still stand on the site, though in a sad and semi-ruined state. The original school was a single room school building, but in 1926, an addition was joined to the west end of the original building. The renovated school accommodated a larger number of students and teachers that occurred after it consolidated with the Hopeview School (see page 65). Water for Peace Valley came from a deep well across from the school house that, in the past, had been used for a sheep camp.

62. PEATH *

The Peath School was located at MCR HH.5 on MCR 23 on the west side of MCR 23, 15½ miles north and 4 miles east of Fort Morgan.

63. PLAINVIEW *

The Plainview School was located in the southwest corner of the intersection of extended lines of MCR FF and MCR 9, 7 miles due north of Weldona. An aerial photograph of this site reveals foundation works that are typical of those provided for a one-room country school and cloakroom. However, there is no ready access to this location on private property which is one mile from either of the nearest County Roads.

64. PLEASANT RIDGE

The Pleasant Ridge School was located on the northwest corner of the intersection of MCR E and MCR 23, 13 miles south and 4 miles east of Fort Morgan.

65. PUGH

The Pugh School was located in the southwest corner of the intersection of MCR S and MCR 8, 2 miles north and 4 miles east of Wiggins. The Pugh School was opened in 1912 as one of the five schools built that year in the southwest part of the County by District 12 for the total sum of $2,000.

66. RAUTH *

The Rauth School was located on MCR I at 25.5, near the center of section 20-1N-56W on the north side of MCR I, 8½ miles south and 6½ miles east of Fort Morgan.

State Teacher's Diploma (1932)
Awarded to Margaret Louise Warner on February 7th, 1932

… Diploma.

… OF THE STATE OF COLORADO.

… sents may come, Greeting:

… use Warner is hereby granted this
… ls of Colorado until February 7th, 1932.
… rding to law.
… nd the seal of the Department of Education,
… seventh day of February
… must be made before date of expiration.

Katherine L. Craig
PRESIDENT STATE BOARD OF EDUCATION.

Carroll Armstrong
SECRETARY STATE BOARD OF EDUCATION.

67. REED *

The Reed School was located at MCR 3.4 on MCR G at 3400 MCR G on the north side of MCR G, 10 miles south and ½ mile east of Wiggins. The Reed School was moved from its original site, re-opened as a school on its new site and re-named the "Old Trail School". It was purchased in 1964 by the Wiggins Historical Society in Wiggins and as the result of the local Historical Society's efforts, has been registered in the State and National Register of Historic Places as the "Old Trail School" (see page 81).

Sample Question from Teacher Examination — Educational Psychology section — true or false?

The neuron is the unit of the nervous system

As one learns, the number of brain cells increases.

Answers: T, F

Did you know . . .

The schools were lit by kerosene and gas lanterns. The students programs were music, plays, and readings.

Every student had a part in the program. Santa Claus arrived giving each child a sack filled with candy, fruit and nuts — this was a special treat!

68. RIVERSIDE *

Riverside School (1937)
Image courtesy of Kay Coffin

The Riverside School site is mapped 3½ miles due north of Hillrose on the east side of MCR 32 at MCR Z.5. There is no evidence of a school from an aerial photograph of the site. School District No. 16 (Part of Weld County – became part of District No. 1 Snyder.) In 1916 — District No. 16, No. 18, and No. 19 withdrew from the No. 1 Snyder District. Snyder wanted to consolidate in 1917, but the effort was bitterly opposed and defeated. In 1937, children from Coss (see page 52) and North Star (see page 78) were bussed to Gilliland (see page 58).

Sample Question from Teacher Examination
Grammar and Composition section —
Arrange the sentences in proper order by writing no the blank the numbers of the sentences in the order in which they should appear.

.... (1) Many people own two-family flats, living in one and renting the other. (2) Home ownership has its advantages from a financial point of view. (3) The rent pays the expenses of the home and sometimes more. (4) When a person owns this type of home, he is very well situated.

Answer: 2,1,3,4

Did you know . . .

Getting ready for the school program meant a girl had to have curls.

The hair was washed and wrapped with strips of rags left in overnight.

(Yes, she slept on the rags.)

The next day, and for a week after she had long curls.

69. ROCK CREEK *

The Rock Creek School was located at MCR F.5 on MCR 1 on the east side, 10½ miles south and 3 miles west of Wiggins. Around 1909, local residents donated money for the building of a frame school at the Hoyt School site. When the need, in 1918, arose for larger facilities, the new Hoyt school building was constructed at its present site on County Road B. The original small wood frame Hoyt School was moved from the Hoyt site to become the Rock Creek School.

70. ROCK SPRINGS

The Rock Springs School was located on MCR 21 at MCR BB.75 on the west side of MCR 21, 9¾ miles north and 2 miles east of Fort Morgan.

> Sample Question from Teacher Examination
> — English Literature section
>
> The earliest of the following writers was (a) Bede, (b) Chaucer, (c) Shakespeare, (d) Spencer, (e) Wyatt.
>
> *Answer: A*

71. SAN ARROYA

San Arroyo School (1905)
Teacher—A.H. Cutler

The San Arroya School was located in the southwest corner of the intersection of MCR K and MCR 13, 7 miles south and 5 miles west of Fort Morgan.

72. S.E. GARY *

The S.E. Gary School was located at the intersection of MCR Rd. C and MCR 34, 15 miles south and 6 miles east of Brush. The one-room school was built 3 miles east of the South Gary School in 1912. It was known as the Southeast Gary School.

73. SNYDER

Snyder School (c. 1895)

According to a paper by Erma Lake submitted for *History of East Morgan County*:

> The first school was held in Snyder in about 1871 in a three room dwelling painted pink. It was located a quarter of a mile west of the present town site. School was held at this location until 1881 when the Union Pacific Railroad was completed. Some time after 1881, a second school was built, located on the east edge of the present town, which served the community until 1901. It was called the "McGill School." The third school was built in 1901. It was located in the northwest part of town. In 1916 the fourth school was built to remedy an overcrowding at the third school. The latest school was called the "White Building."

As years passed, many of the one and two room school houses located a few miles apart north and south of the river in the Snyder District community were merged and became the Snyder Consolidated School District. In 1918, the first two grades of high school were added to the school curriculum, and in 1920 and 1921 the fifth school, known as the "Brick Building" was built to house the Junior and Senior High School. The class of 1925 was the first class to complete four years of high school in the new building. In 1965, the Snyder Junior and Senior High Schools were closed and the students bussed to Brush. The grade school followed two years later in 1967.

74. SUNBURG

The Sunburg School was located on MCR JJ at 34.5 on the north side of MCR JJ, 10 miles north and 5¼ miles east of Snyder. There are remnants on the site including parts of a foundation structure measuring 18 feet in width east to west, what appears to be a cistern, and a playground pole just across Road JJ. The school yard is easily discernable from the surrounding prairie.

Did you know . . .

In every school yard were two outhouses near the fence (boys & girls).

In each outhouse was a flat wooden box that held a Sears or Montgomery Ward Catalog to be used as toilet paper.

Ants, wasps, and flies were ever present occupants.

75. SUNNYSIDE

Sunnyside School (c. 1900)

The Sunnyside School was located in the far northwest corner of the County, in the northwest corner of the intersection of MCR II and the MCR 8 line — 10 miles north and 1 mile west of Weldona. The picturesque name Sunnyside was selected in tribute to the optimism shared by the early homesteaders. The Sunnyside School was built in 1915. In 1965, District No. 14 and the Sunnyside School District were merged with the Weldon Valley School District — although its students were attending school in Weldona before the effective date of the reorganization.

Sample Question from Teacher Examination
Writing section —

The appraisal of the pupil's handwriting should be done
(a) primarily by the teacher, (b) by the other pupils of the class,
(c) by the pupil himself with the help of the teacher.

Answer: A

76. S.W. GARY *

The S.W. Gary School was located just north and east of the intersection of MCR C and MCR 31, 15 miles south and 3 miles east of Brush. It appears that its foundation and basement is still there, and what are believed to be pieces of the original white siding were discovered on the site in November of 2014.

Sample Question from Teacher Examination — General History section — mark those that are correct.

Feudalism

.... (a) was a social relationship based on the possession of land.

.... (b) grew up because of the weakness of government.

.... (c) disappeared when national governments grew up.

.... (d) made the king more powerful.

.... (e) was a relationship between the Pope and the bishops.

Answer: A

Did you know . . .

Students owned an autograph book in which classmates wrote a verse or a bit of nonsense

*— I wish you luck,
I wish you joy,
I wish your first a baby boy,
And when his hair begins to curl,
I wish you then a baby girl.*

Love Ann

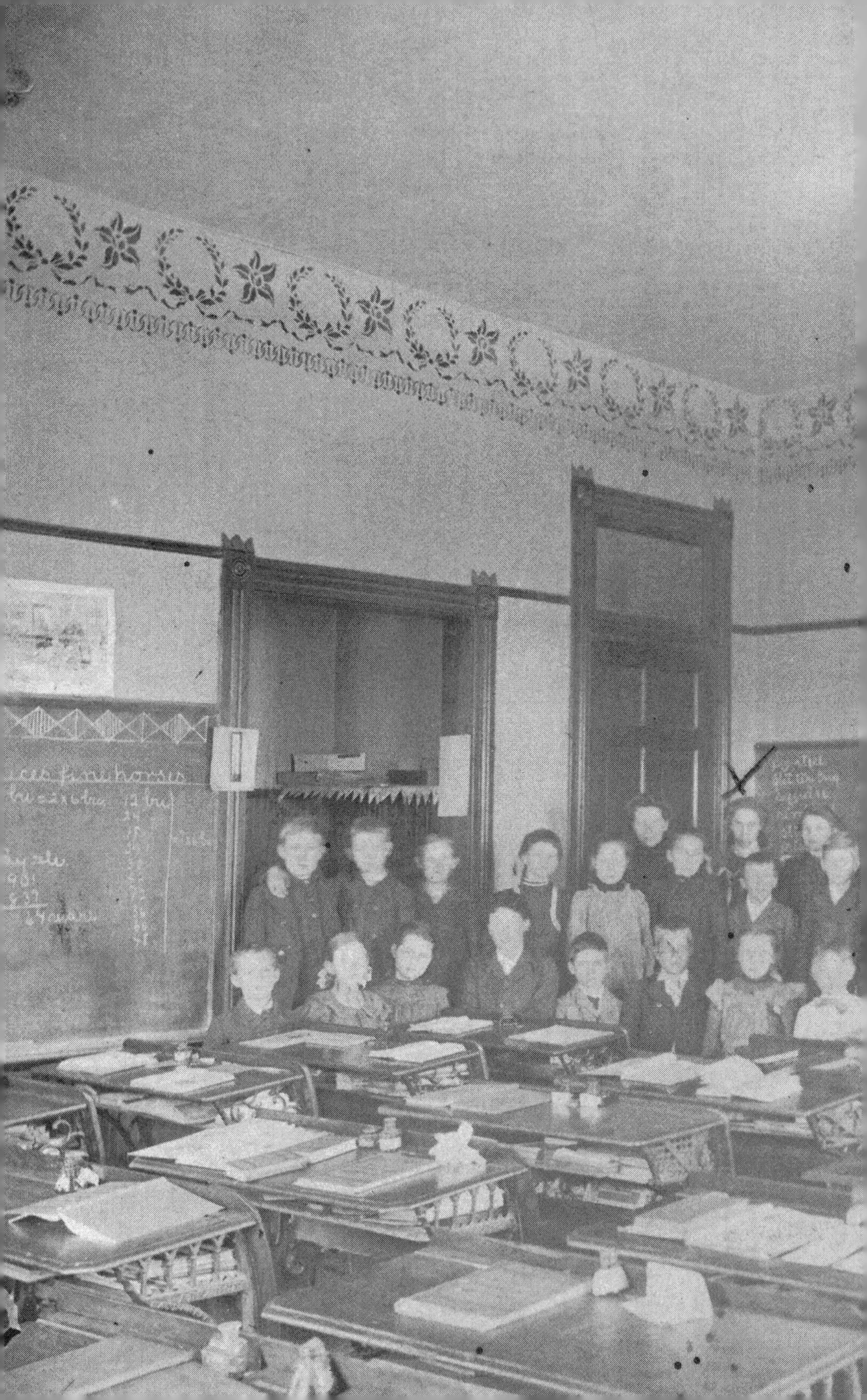

Unknown School Interior (c. 1910)
'X' over pupil is identified as Maude Carroll Hammond

77. TWOMBLY *

Twombly School (1915)
Image Courtesy of the Library of Congress

The Twombly school, named for Hurd Twombly, was located in the southeast corner of the intersection of MCR S and MCR 25, 2 miles due west of Brush on MCR S. The 1913 Atlas places the school on MCR R.5 or US Hwy 34 at MCR 25, 2 miles west of Brush at a location which is ½ mile south of the County Map site.

Hurd Warren Twombly (1880)
Pioneer, rancher, Sherriff, Morgan County Commissioner, and Banker.

78. UNION

The Union School was located on MCR W.7 at MCR X.95 in Union, at a site approximately 3½ miles north and 1¼ miles east of Snyder. After the school was closed due to consolidation, the school was moved approximately 3½ miles west and 6 miles north of its original site to its present location on MCR 31, just south of MCR FF, where it has been made into a private home.

> Sample Question from Teacher Examination
> — Algebra section
>
> The product of (a-b) (a+b)
>
> The square of (a-b)
>
> The square of the sum of two numbers.
>
> Answers: a^2-b^2, $a^2-2ab+b^2$, $(a+b)^2$

79. UPPER WILDCAT *

2015

The Upper Wildcat School is located in north-central Morgan County on MCR 21 south of its intersection with MCR Y and on the West side of MCR 21, 5¾ miles north and 3 miles east of Fort Morgan. Obviously, the schoolhouse, which still sits at or close to, its original location, has been modified for use as a garage and storage building. It still contains a blackboard and the original heating stove.

> Sample Questions from Teacher Examination
> — Elementary Science and Agriculture section — true or false?
>
> Cold prevents the growth of bacteria
>
> Silver bromide changes its composition when exposed to light
>
> Temperature is the intensity or degree of heat.
>
> Answers: F, T, T

80. VALLEY VIEW

The Valley View School was located in the northwest corner of the intersection of MCR K and MCR 2, 7 miles south and 2 miles east of Fort Morgan.

81. VALLEY VIEW *

The second Valley View School was located on MCR DD at MCR 28.4 on the north side of MCR DD, 6 miles north and ½ to ¾ mile west of Snyder.

Sample Question from Teacher Examination — History of the United States section — true or false?

The Second Continental Congress arranged for army supplies and made Washington commander-in-chief

The Declaration of Independence was written by Hamilton

Answers: T, F

Did you know . . .

Many students ended their education with the 8th Grade Graduation.

Ceremonies were held with students dressed in their finest.

Diplomas were awarded. Some then continued on to high school.

FORT MORGAN PUBLIC SCHOOLS

R. R. BROURINK, Superintendent

Fort Morgan, Colorado

School Year 194*2* - 194*3*

Report of *King, Gayland's Dog*
Age *5* Grade *Special* School *Victory*
Teacher *Miss Dorothy Acre*
Days Absent *Several* Days Attendance *Plenty*
Times Tardy *Several*

PROMOTION CERTIFICATE

This is to certify that

King, Gayland's Dog

has completed the work of the *6th* grade

and is entitled to promotion to the *7th* grade

Date *May 28, 1943*

Dorothy M. Acre
Principal

A Fort Morgan public schools report card for the school year 1942-1943 made out for "King", Gayland Coup's dog, Age 5, Grade Special, School Victory, Teacher Miss Dorothy Acre." Showed days absent — several, days attendance: Plenty, and times tardy: Several. King completed 6th grade work and was entitled to promotion to the 7th grade, dated May 28, 1943 by Dorothy M. Acre, Principal.

82. VICTORY

Baseball at Victory School. (c. 1940)

Victory School was located in the Northwest corner of the intersection of MCR DD and MCR 23, 11 miles north 5 miles east of Fort Morgan. Joyce Simpson, a former student, in a 2014 memo, has provided the following information:

> Victory School was a one room school with one teacher for all eight grades. A room was added for a stage, and a place for the teacher to live. It was heated with a coal stove and water was pumped from a well in front of the school.
>
> Cliff Thomas served as a "bus driver" using his own car. He would pick up the children on the roads north of the school and then leave them at school while he picked up the rest of us living south of the school.
>
> Around 1939 or 1940 Lucille Coup cooked and brought hot lunches to the school. I remember they brought them by team and wagon sometimes because the roads were snowed in, and maintainers didn't come out that far to open them. Some of the teachers were – Ada Crawford, Grace Barkley, Cathryn Glassey, Ruth Powel (from Orchard) and Dorothy Acre.
>
> The school was the gathering place for dinners, pie socials, card parties and Sunday School.
>
> To attend High School, kids either rode a horse about 3 to 5 miles to catch a bus into Fort Morgan for High School, or arranged to rent a room in town.
>
> In the 1950's, the REA brought electric lines in and telephone lines were hooked to the REA poles. The school thus got electricity and a pay phone.
>
> When Victory was no longer needed for a school it was sold to the Morgan County and was moved west to Highway 52 to be used as a house for the maintenance man. It has since been moved from there.

Did you know . . .

Saying it was "only a mile to school" might have been true if a person cut through cow pastures - crawling under barbwire fences while keeping a watchful eye out for any ill-tempered bull that might roam the pasture.

And watch out for snakes.

83. WANDEL

The Wandel School was located on the west side of the MCR 26 (line) at Z.4 (line), 7½ miles north and 1 mile west of Brush. The site is now within the confines of the Riverside Irrigation District's Vancil Reservoir.

84. WELCOME HOLLOW

The Welcome Hollow School was located on the north side of MCR II at MCR 28, 11 miles north and ¾ mile west of Snyder.

85. WELDON

The Weldon School was located at the intersection of MCR U.5 and MCR 8.4 at 8400 MCR U.5, 3½ miles south and ¼ mile west of Weldona.

Sample Question from Teacher Examination — Sanitation and Hygiene section — true or false?

Alcohol is produced by bacteria.

Answer: F

86. WELDON VALLEY

Weldona School (c. 1900)

The first Weldon Valley School was a one-room school built in 1887 in the west edge of the town then named "Duel", and is now part of a private residence at that location. In 1897, the two-room school was built along the north side of Highway 144 about half way between the alley separating Main Street and Warren Street.

Nine years later, in 1906, a bond proposal to build a new, larger school was approved. In 1908, William Putnam agreed to give the necessary land to build the new school. Louis Collier of Weldona was successful bidder to construct the new school. A 62 foot by 30 foot, two story brick school was built to serve eight grades at a cost of $7,750. With completion of the new school, the 1897 two-room school was moved to the west part of town to be made into a dwelling. The first of many changes to be made to the 1908 building over the years, was embarked on in 1917 adding four rooms, an assembly hall, and a third floor.

The Weldon Valley School District was reorganized in 1956. This merged the Weldona School with the schools serving the Orchard and Goodrich School Districts. The three school districts were united at that time. A bond election was held to raise funds to add to the school in Weldona— a new elementary wing, gymnasium/auditorium, locker room, cafeteria and kitchen were built for the new school year in September. The 1908 building was given a facelift, and the third floor was removed. All of the Morgan County schools and school districts were completely reorganized in 1963. At that time all of the schools were merged, and the county's rural schools were consolidated by their incorporation into four surviving school districts. The Weldon Valley District, re-designated Weldon Valley RE-20, was one of the four surviving districts.

87. WEST NILE

The West Nile School was located at MCR M, in the northeast corner of the intersection of MCR M and the line of MCR 2, 4 miles south and 2 miles west of Wiggins. The West Nile School opened in 1912 as one of the five schools built that year in the southwest part of the County by District No. 12 for the total sum of $2,000.

Wiggins School Bus (c. 1918)
Mable Paulsen, Kellen Kolberg, and Ellen Paulsen

88. WIGGINS

The Wiggins School is located in the Town of Wiggins, formerly known as the Town of Corona. The Wiggins community was established in 1882 as the Burlington railroad depot of Corona. Around 1900, Corona was renamed in honor of Oliver P. Wiggins, who served as a guide and scout for Captain John C. Fremont, on some of his explorations through northern Colorado in the 1840s. He also accompanied Kit Carson for 12 years on his expeditions.

89. WILDCAT

The Wildcat School was located on MCR W at MCR 24.6 on the south side of MCR W, 4 miles north and 2½ miles west of Brush. In 1930, a school bus from Morey School was sent to Wildcat to relieve the overcrowed conditions at the school.

90. WILLET

Willet School was located in the northeast corner of the intersection of MCR S and MCR 12, 6 miles due west of Fort Morgan on the Long Bridge Road.

> Sample Question from Teacher Examination — School Law section — true or false?
>
> Directors of school districts are appointed by the state superintendent.
>
> The state board of education consists of five members.
>
> *Answers: T, T*

> **Did you know...**
>
> Many schools had water trucked in and stored in a cistern.
>
> The cisterns were cleaned yearly and lots of dirt was found in the bottom.
>
> Those at the school shared water and a dipper (cup).

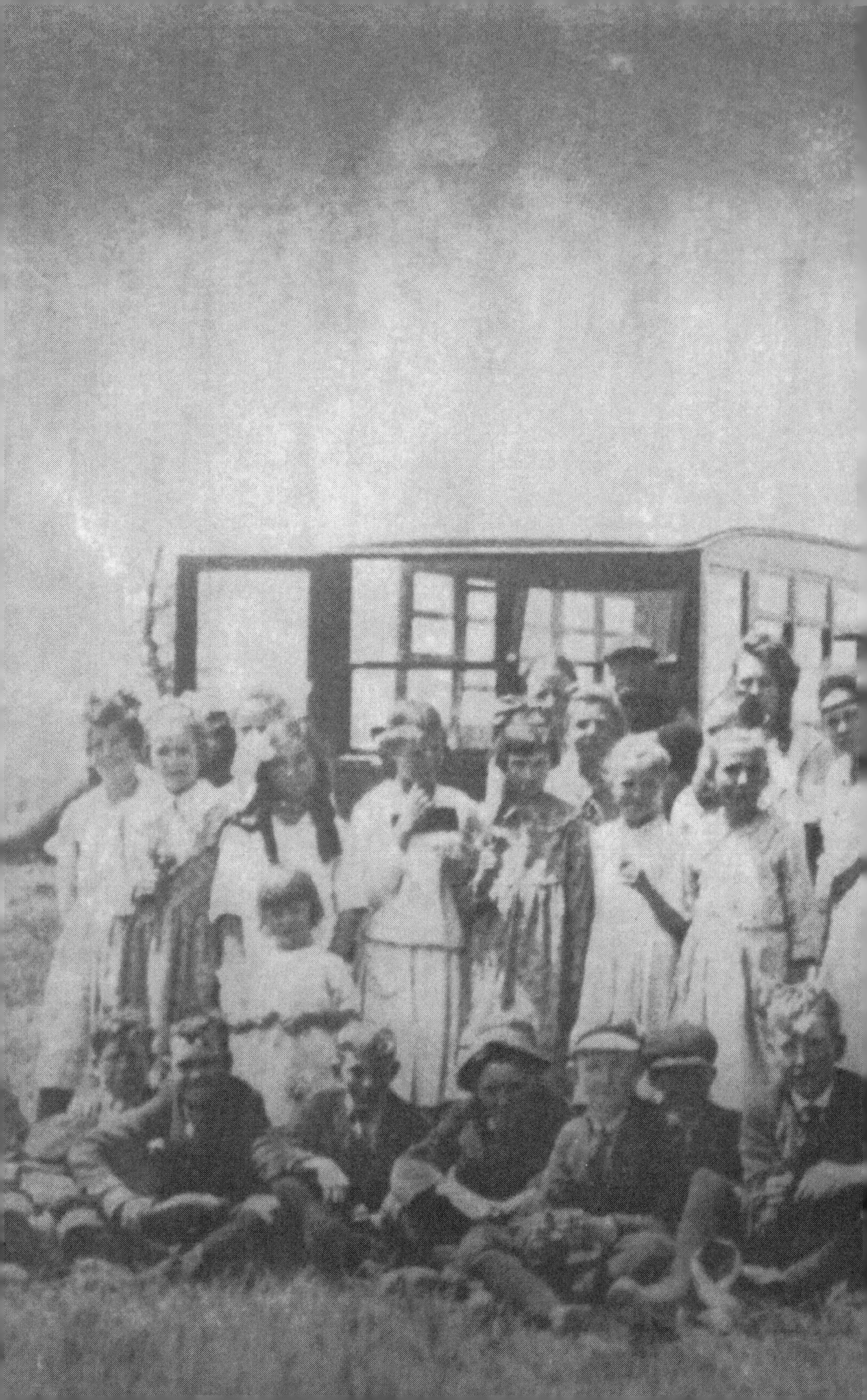

Wiggins School Children on an Outing (c. 1918)

91. WILLIAMS *

Williams School (1915)
Image courtesy of the Library of Congress

The Williams School was located in the southwest corner of the intersection of MCR Q and MCR 25, which is two miles south and three miles west of Brush. There is still some evidence of the school lot and grounds at that location just north of the Pawnee Plant Reservoir. From information supplied by Katherine George — *History of East Morgan County*, we learn:

> ... that the School was named for a Jack Williams and that in 1906 the school enrollment was thirty-five pupils. In 1919 thirty-five children were enrolled and were taught by Dorothy Finney. Another Williams teacher, Ralph W. Kiefer, taught at a salary of $57.50 plus $2.50 for janitorial duties. At the time, men teachers received an average of $5.00 to $10.00 more per month than women teachers.

Reportedly, one teacher traveled to Williams school nearly the whole year riding a bike, and another teacher traveled there by horse and buggy in "real up-town style."

---

92. WORK *

The Work School site was located in the southeast corner of the intersection of MCR Q and MCR 16, 1 mile south and 2 miles west of Fort Morgan.

MAPPED BUT UNIDENTIFIED SCHOOLS

93. *

A school site is located on the northwest corner of the intersection of MCR H and 16, 10 miles south and 1 mile west of Fort Morgan. There is a structure on or near the site that could have been a school building.

94.

A school site is located at MCR 13 at MCR P.5, on the east side of MCR 13, 1½ miles south and 5 miles west of Fort Morgan.

95. *

A School site is located on the south side of MCR JJ at MCR 34.5, 12 miles north and 5½ miles east of Snyder. There is no evidence of a school from an aerial photograph of the site; however, an obvious variance in the natural vegetation appears to indicate the location of the school grounds.

FORT MORGAN PUBLIC SCHOOLS
Fort Morgan, Colorado
School Year
Report of
Age
Grade
School
Teacher
Days Absent
Days Attendance
Times Tardy
PROMOTION CERTIFICATE
This is to certify that
has completed the work of the
and is entitled to promotion to the
Date
OUTLINE MAP OF
MORGAN COUNTY
COLORADO

Dec. '34   M.B. Gill

First School in Morgan County

The first school in Morgan county was held in a *small one-story frame building* on Clifton street Brush by a Mr. Allen. Miss Della Brown was the first teacher, assuming her duties in 1883. She taught about three terms in this building.

A school district embracing all the county south of the river (Weld co.) was organized in 1884, and the county superintendent was A.K. Packard. Mr. Packard was Congregational preacher in Greeley at the time and many young couples went to Packard to be married in this early day. Supt. Packard appointed John T. Wylie, T.J. Smith, and Milton Dunkell as the first board of school directors.

At the first school election J.P. Kimsey was elected president and Mrssrs. M.B. Parker and W.H. Black as members of the school board.

Following is a list of scholars attending school under Miss Brown:

Gilbert Nelson, Pearl Parker, Eugene Parker, Bart Parker, Jennie Kimsey, Nellie Cheadle, Fred Cheadle, Mollie Smith, D. Smith, George Smith, Louise Dixon, Nina Dixon, Myrtle Clark, Nellie Swanson, Harry Kram, George Litch, Ella Litch, Hattie Kram, Nellie Kram, and Edith Kram.

The district missed being no. 1. because of a few people who had interests in Snyder, holding back the Brush application until Snyder assured the first number.

****

Facsimile of Research Paper (1934)
Information is from Mark Gill who was obtaining interviews for the Works Progress Administration (W.P.A.).

XII.
RECENTLY DISCOVERED RURAL SCHOOLS

DELLA BROWN SCHOOL

The first school incorporated into a newly formed Brush School District in 1889 was the Della Brown School, which had been previously established in the town of Brush in 1883. For whatever reason, the Della Brown School was omitted from the inventory of Morgan County Schools numbered and located upon Morgan County's 1976 Reference Map of School Locations. Olivia Hansen from *History of East Morgan County* relates:

> ... The small one-room frame school house was located at what is now 103 Clifton - at the corner of Clifton and Railway Street. It was built by a Mr. Allen. The first teacher was Miss Della Brown. Her salary was $35.00 per month. The School building ... still sits in its original location.

Hansen continues:

> A school district embracing all the county (Weld co.) south of the river was organized in 1884, and the county superintendent was A.K. Packard. He appointed John T. Wylie, T.J. Smith and Milton Dunkell as the first board of school directors.
>
> At the first school election J.P. Kimsey was elected president and Mrs. M.B. Parker and W.H. Black as members of the school board.
>
> Following is a list of scholars attending school under Miss Brown: Gilbert Nelson, Pearl Parker, Eugene Parker, Bert Parker, Jennie Kimsey, Nellie Cheadle, Fred Cheadle, Mollie Smith, D. Smith, George Smith, Louise Dixon, Nina Dixon, Myrtle Clark, Nellie Swanson, Harry Kram, George Litch, Ella Litch, Hattie Kram, Nellie Kram, and Edith Kram.
>
> The district missed being No. 1 because of a few people who had interests in Snyder, holding back the Brush application until Snyder assured the first number.

LIBERTY SCHOOL

In the *History of East Morgan County* Katherine George recalls, The Liberty School, established in 1906, has been described as being located three miles south of the Nine Mile Corner, or five miles east of the Nine Mile Corner on the old highway to Akron.

She continues, Eli Mangus donated a corner of his pasture for the school. In 1906 ten children were enrolled; teachers at Liberty included Mamie Wetzbarger, Elizabeth Church and Marge Ely. That building was later moved to Roggen where it is still used as a Nazarene Church.

Floyd Duvall states:

> There was an unused school house west of Nine Mile Corner from across the Beaver Creek not far west of the creek which was available. The men from the Liberty neighborhood

moved the schoolhouse. When we got the schoolhouse up over the hill east of the Nine Mile Corner a member of the Brush School Board drove out. He said "This is where the school is going to be." I remember just like it was yesterday. Every man was on his feet ready for a fight. The school board member went back to his car and drove off." Of course they continued on to the offered site on the E.B. Mangus half-section which was centrally located in the neighborhood.

Mamie (McAfee) Wetzbarger
History of East Morgan County

LITTLE BEAVER:
No other information

MOON FLAG VALLEY:
No other information

MISSIONARY RIDGE:
No other information

ONE ADDITIONAL UNIDENTIFIED SCHOOL

An unnamed and otherwise unidentified school, not listed and located on the County Map, is, however, located and mapped by the 1913 Standard Atlas. This school was located in the northwest corner of the intersection of MCR T and MCR 15, approximately 1 mile north and 3 miles west of Fort Morgan on or near what is now Co Hwy 144, not far east of the Bijou Creek crossing.

SMITH SCHOOL

The Smith School was built in 1907 on a site one mile west of the 9-mile corner. In order to have enough children to justify the building of the school, five of the Charles H. Smith children, who were then attending Hagan were transferred to the new Smith school. The two teachers at the Smith School were Goldie Anderson (Weimer) and Helen Rose (Anderson). They drove by horse and buggy to the school.

The newest Fort Morgan Middle School is shown here. It opened in 2016.

XIII.

THE END OF THE RURAL SCHOOLS

The first Superintendent of Schools, W. E. Garver, was elected or appointed in 1890. The thirteenth and last Superintendent of Morgan County Schools was Marian Lockwood who served for eighteen years, from 1947 until 1965. In that year a plan for consolidation of the county's schools was completed, and more than fifty-seven years of educating children in Morgan County's rural country schools ended.

It needs to be said, that for all the benefits realized from the closing of the rural schools, it was not done without real social consequence. Nearly every one of those school communities that had endured since homestead days declined — several disappeared. There was no familiar schoolhouse and teacher down the road to send their children to – no schoolhouse for a Saturday night dance – no church meetings – no schoolhouse for Election Day – for Grange meetings – for the 4-H club – for the quilting bee – for the reading group – for those gatherings that are the heart of a community. Is it any wonder that there was real sadness; even tears when the people's schools were removed from those cherished places where they, themselves, went to school, and from the communities where they lived their lives?

AFTERWORD

This book was produced in conjunction with a Fort Morgan Museum exhibit named after the same title.

NEW MUSEUM EXHIBIT
LOOKS AT SCHOOLHOUSE HISTORY

The show includes artifacts, photographs, and satellite images of one room school locations throughout the county.

A new exhibition at the Fort Morgan Museum will offer a glimpse of the important history of one-room schoolhouses in Morgan County. The exhibit will run from Sept. 1 to Dec. 31, 2016 in the Museum's Lower Gallery.

APPENDICES

APPENDIX 1.
LIST OF MORGAN COUNTY SUPERINTENDENTS

The superintendent is an administrator or manager in charge of a number of public schools or a school district. The role and powers of the superintendent varies among areas. One of the most important roles of the board of education is to hire its superintendent.

1889 – 1891 William E. Carver

1892—1893 Samuel A. Wallace

1894-1895 M. E. Lowe

1896-1897 Annie L. P. Gerver

1898-1899 Fay E. Williams

1900-1904 Mattie Clifford

1905-1908 Grace Anderson

1909-1912 Helen Mar Simpson

1913-1916 Anne R. White

1917-1920 Charlie Price Cochran

1921-1932 Laura N. Burchsted

1933-1946 Rose B. Glassey (died Dec. 26, 1946)

1947-1965 Marian Lockwood

APPENDIX 2.
POPULAR GAMES

Anti-I-Over: The object of the game is to throw a ball over the roof of the schoolhouse or woodshed.

Baseball: a ball game played between two teams on a field with a diamond-shaped circuit of four bases.

Fox and Goose: When the fox tags a goose, the goose becomes the fox's pal and chases after the geese. The more fox chasing geese, the harder it becomes to stop falling prey to one of them. The winner is the last goose left standing who then becomes the new fox.

Hop Scotch: A game based on an idea of not treading on lines. The game's English name expresses its object: to hop over the "scotch," a line, or scratch, drawn on the ground. Lines are drawn in a variety of patterns. Spaces in the diagrams are numbered, and they must be traversed in order.

Jacks: A game played with stones, bones, seeds, filled cloth bags, or metal or plastic counters (the jacks), with or without a ball.

Marbles: The object of marble games is to roll, throw, drop, or knuckle marbles against an opponent's marbles, often to knock them out of a pre-scribed area and so win them.

Mother May I: One player plays the "mother." The other players are the "children." To begin the game, the mother stands at one end of a room and turns around facing away, while all the children line up at the other end. The children take turns asking "Mother may I ____?" and makes a movement suggestion. The mother/father either replies "Yes, you may" or "No, you may not do that, but you may _____ instead." The players usually move closer to the mother/father but are sometimes led farther away. Even if the mother makes an unfavorable suggestion, the child must still perform it. The first of the children to reach the location of the mother wins the game.

Skipping (Jumping) Rope: A game played by individuals or teams with a piece of rope, which may have handles attached at each end.

Tag: A player who is "it" chases the other players, trying to touch one of them, thereby making that person "it."

Bibliography

Baughn, James. "Historic and Notable Landmarks of the U.S." *Rural School Buildings in Colorado MPS*. Contributors, 2002. Web. 3 Sept. 2016.

Bell, L. (2007, June). School Sections: Cash Cows or Environmental Resources. *North Forty News & Fossil Creek Current*.

Carlson, E. and Pauls, J. and Brethauer K. (1994). *A View of Orchard: Roots and All*. Boulder, Colo.: Johnson Printing.

Colorado. Department of Public Instruction (1921). *Colorado State Course of Study in Education*. Denver, CO.: State of Colorado.

Colorado Young Citizens League (1940). *History of Morgan County*. Fort Morgan, CO.

Coup, Gayland. "Victory School." Interview. 07 July 2015: n.

Downing, Thelma. *Experiences of Thelma (Kentopp Downing)*. Fort Morgan: Fort Morgan Museum, 01 Sept. 2016. PDF.

"First School in Morgan County." Interview by Mark B. Gill. *WPA Interviews* 1935: 183. Print.

Friends of East Morgan County, Colorado including papers by Alice Colwell, Katherine George, Olivia Hansen, Emma Lake, Helen Underwood, Mamie (McAfee) Wetzbarger. *The History of East Morgan County, Colorado*. Dallas: Curtis Media Corporation, 1987. Print.

Geo. A. Ogle & Co. *Standard Atlas of Morgan County Colorado*. [map]. Scale 7/20 of 1 inch to 1 mile. Chicago, IL: 1913.

Bibliography

Groves, H. S., ed. "Morgan County." *Ranch and Range* Dec. 1902: 1-20. Print.

Johnson, Wes "Glenwood School." Interview. 05 June 2015.

Lewis, Inez Johnson—State Superintendent of Public Instruction. *Examination for Teachers for Third, Second, and First Grand Certificates.* Denver Colorado, 1936

Lumpkin, Bob, and Lloyd Ladd. *Morgan County Country Schools 1884-1965.* [map]. Fort Morgan: Morgan County Commissioners Office, 1974. Print.

"Morgan County, Colorado." *Fort Morgan Times* 1 Sept. 1899: n. pag. Print.

Persell, Diana J. Edwardson and Michele R. Webb (1994). *My Folks and the One-Room Schoolhouse.* Topeka, KS: Capper Press.

Shaffer, Ray (1978). *A Guide to Places on the Colorado Prairie 1540-1975.* Boulder, CO.: Pruett Publishing Company.

Simpson, Joyce. *Victory School.* Rep. Fort Morgan: n.p., 2014. 1-2. Print.

Suki. "Teacher Contracts from the 1920's." *Certificate Street*. N.p., 22 Oct. 2009. Web. 18 July 2016.

United States. Census Bureau. Washington: GPO, 1890. Print.

Walters, Hildred and Lorraine Young (1974), Colorado Prairie Tales. Scottsbluff, NE: The Business Farmer Printing Co.

Index
Italics denotes illustration

A

Acre, Dorothy, 106, 107
Adena, Edna, 36, *36, 37, 38-39, 40*
Adena Sod Schoolhouse 40
Adean Sod Interior 82
Adena Lions Club, 36
Adena Schools, 36-40, 82
Allen, Mr. 119
Ambrose School, 41, *41*
Ambrose School Interior 7
Anderson, Goldie (Weimer), 121
Anderson (Searles – Anderson), 64
Antelope Bend School, 42, *42*
Antelope Springs School, 43, *43*
Antelope Valley School, 44, *44*
Atlas (1913) 4, *32-33*

B

Barkley, Grace, 107
Baseball at Victory School 23
Beaver Creek, 31, 120
Bijou Creek, 31, 66, 121
Beuttler School, 45,
Bijou View School, 46, *46*
Black, W.H., 120
Bleasdales, Alice, 69
Brammer School, 47, *47*
Brown, Miss Della, 119
Bruen School, 48,
Brush Municipal Park, 68
Brush School Board, 120
Brush School District #1, 7
Burlington depot - Corona, 110

C

Carson, Kit, 110
Center School, 48
Centerville School, 49, *49*
Chace School, 50
Cheadle, Fred, 120
Cheadle, Nellie, 120
Church, Elizabeth, 120
Clark, Myrtle, 120
Class Three Teacher Certificate, 9
Collier, Louis, 109
Columbine School, 50
Colwell, Alice, 51, 69
Colwell, C.I. 51
Colwell School, 51, *51*
Corona, 110
Coss School, 52, 58, 93
County Map identifies 96 sites, 25
County Seat, Fort Morgan, 31
County Superintendent of Schools, 2, 22, 45, 123
Coup, Gayland, 106
Coup, Lucille, 107
Crawford, Ada, 107

D

Della Brown School, 119, *119*
Dixon, Louise, 120
Dixon, Nina, 120
Dodd School, 52
Downing, Thelma (Kentopp), 21-22
Duel School, 109
Dunkell, Milton, 120
Dust Bowl Days, 10
Duvall, Floyd, 120

Index

Italics denotes illustration

E

Elementary certificates, 7
Ely, Marge, 120
Teacher—Lura Elkerton 14
Emerson School, 52

F

55 Ranch, 87
Fairview School, 51, 53, *53*
"Fight", schoolhouse name, 25
Finney, Dorothy, 114
First teacher's examination, 9
Fort Morgan, Colo. 30-31
Fort Morgan Middle school 2016 122
Fort Morgan School District #3, 7
Fort Morgan Times, *26*, 31
Fremont, Captain John C., 110

G

Garfield School, 56
Garver, W.E., 2, 123
Gary General Store, 99
Gary Post Office, 56-57, 99
Gary School, 56
Gary NE School, 76, *76*
Gary SE, 95
Gary SW, 99
George, Katherine, 64, 69, 114, 120
Ghost Children v
Gilland, Sam, 58
Gilland School, 52, 58, *58,* 78, 93
Gilland School District, 58
Glassey, Cathryn, 107

Glencoe School, 59
George, Kay, and John Glenn rode Horseback 12
Grant School 54-55
Glenwood School, 60, *60*
Goodrich, G.W. 61
Goodrich School, 61, *61-62*
Google Earth Imaging, vii
Grandview School, 64
Gregg, Efay (Nelson), 69

H

Hagan, Mr., 64
Hagan School, 64, 68, 121
Hansen, Olivia, 119
Hayford School, 65
Hilltop School, 65
Homestead Act of 1862, 1
Hopeview School, 65, 88
Hoyt Community Center, 66
Hoyt School, 66, *66*, 94
Hunt, Jim, 64
Hunter's Hill School, 67
Hurley, Mrs. J.M., 69
Hurley School, 67

J

Johnson, Wes, 60
Johnson School, 67

K

Kiefer, Ralph, 114
Kimsey, J.P., 120
Kimsey, Jennie, 120
Knearl School, 68, *70-71*

Index

Italics denotes illustration

Knearl, William, 68
Kolberg, Kellen, 110
Kram, Edith, 120
Kram, Harry, 120
Kram, Hattie, 120
Kram, Nellie, 120

L

Ladd, Lloyd, 4
Lake, Erma, 96
Lake View, 69
Lauck, Henry, 51
Liberty School, 68, 69, 120-121
Light, Charles, 69
Light School, 68, *69*
Abraham Lincoln xii
Litch, Ella, 120
Litch, George, 120
Lockwood, Marian, 123
Long Meadow Community Club Building, 72
Long Meadow School, 72, *72*
Longs Peak School, 73
Lower Wildcat School, 73
Lumpkin, Bob, 4
Lung, L.F., 28

M

Mac's School, 74
Mangus, E.B. 121
Mangus, Eli, 120
McCook Junior College, 21
McCook Nebraska, 21
McGill School, 96
McGuffery Readers, 42
Miller School, 74
Missionary Ridge School, 121
Missouri Valley School, 74
Moon Flag Valley School, 121
Morey School, 75, *75,* 111
Morgan County iii, 2
1913 Morgan County Atlas 5
Morgan County Statistics, 31
Morgan County Superintendent of Schools, 64
Morey, A.J., 75
Mura, Miss Helen, 27
Helen Mura Gravesite 26
Museum, Brush Municipal, 68
Musgrave Homestead 24

N

National Register of Historic Places, 29, 81, 92
Nazarene Church, Roggen, 120
Nelson, Gilbert, 120
New Deal era federal relief program, 67
Nine Mile corner, 64, 120
NO. 2 School, 77
NO. 4 School, 77
Normal Training Classes, 9
North Prairie Style, 3, *6*
North Star School, 27-28, 58 78, *78,* 93
Normal Training, 7

Index

Italics denotes illustration

O

O'Dell School, 79, *79*
OK School 80, *80*
Old Trail School, *28*, 29, 81, *81*, 92
Orchard School, 82, *82*
Orchard Sod Schoolhouse 83, 84-85
Orchard (Sod School -1884), 83
Ott School, 86
Overland Trail, 81
Oxen at Weldon Valley 24

P

Packard, A.K., 120
Parker, Bert, 120
Parker, Mrs. M.B., 120
Parker, Pearl, 120
Park School, 86,
Parker, Eugene, 120
Parson, Jennie, 52
Paul School, 87, *87*
Paul family, 87
Paulsen, Ellen, 110
Paulsen, Mabel, 110
Pawnee Plant Reservoir, 114
Pay, 16
Peace Valley School, 65, 88, *88*
Peath School, 89
Peterson, Ed, 78
Picinic, School 78
Plainview School, 89
Pleasant Prairie School, 50
Pleasant Ridge School, 89
Plowhead, Miss L., 51
Powel, Ruth, 107
"Prairie Glen" School, 58

Prairie Schools in Morgan County, 1
Prairie Schools, two major varieties, 3
Population, 5, 25
Pugh School, 89
Putnam, William, 109

R

Rauth School, 89
REA, 107
Reed School, 81, 92
Report Card 50
Report Card for King 106
Re-named schoolhouses, 25
Reed, George, 81
Facsimile of Researh Paper 1934 118
Ripley, Hazel, 50
Riverside School, 52, 58, 92, 93, *93*
Rock Creek School, 94
Rock Springs School, 94
Rose, Helen (Anderson), 69, 121

S

Sailsbury, Ben, 27
San Arroya School, 95, *95*
School Bus 90-91
School Districts: #1 Snyder, 7, 52, 93, #2 Brush, 7, 64, 68, 69, #3 Fort Morgan, 7, #4 Weld, 7, #5 Hillrose, #5 Morgan County, #7 Gary, #7 Weld School District, 83, #10 Glencoe, #12, 45, 74, 89, 110, #14 Pleasant Prairie, #16, 52, #16 (Part of Weld County),

Index

Italics denotes illustration

93 #18, 93, #19, 93, #41 Brush, 7, #95 Weld County, Brush, 119, Goodrich, 109, Orchard, 109, RE-2 Brush, 57, 64, RE-20 Weldon Valley, 109, Sunnyside, 98, Weld County, 120, Weldon Valley, 109

School No. 9 District No. 3 8
School No. 9 District No. 3 (2) 11

Schools: Adena, 36-40, 82, Ambrose, 41, Antelope Bend, 42, Antelope Springs, 43, Antelope Valley, 44, Beuttler, 45, Bijou View, 46, Brammer, 47, Brick Building (Snyder), 96, Bruen, 48, Center, 48, Centerville, 49, Chace, 50, Columbine, 50, Colwell, 51, Coss, 52, 58, 93, Della Brown, 119, Dodd, 52, Duel, 109, Emerson, 52, Fairview, 51, 53 "Fight", 25, Garfield, 56, Gary, 56, Gilliland, 52, 58, 78, 93, Glencoe, 59, Glenwood, 60, Goodrich, 61, Grandview, 64, Hagan, 64, 68, 121, Hayford, 65, Hilltop, 65, Hopeview, 65, 88, Hoyt, 66, 94, Hunter's Hill, 67, Hurley, 67, Johnson, 67, Knearl, 68, Lake View, 69, Light, 68, Liberty, 68, 69, 120-121, Long Meadow, 72, Longs Peak, 73, Lower Wildcat, 73, Mac's, 74, McGill, 96, Midway, 74, Miller, 74, Missionary Ridge, 121, Missouri Valley, 74, Moon Flag Valley, 121, Morey, 75, 111, N.E. Gary, 76, NO. 2, 77, NO. 4, 77, North Star, 27-28, 58, 78, 93, O'Dell, 79, OK, 80, Old Trail School, 29, 81, 92, Orchard, 82, Orchard (Sod-1884), 83, Ott, 86, Park, 86, Paul, 87, Peace Valley, 65, 88, Peath, 89, Plainview, 89, Pleasant Prairie, 50, Pleasant Ridge, 89, "Prairie Glen", 58, Pugh, 89, Rauth, 89, Reed, 81, 92, Riverside, 52, 58, 92, 93, Rock Creek, 94, Rock Springs, 94, San Arroya, 95, SE Gary, 95, South Gary, 95, Smith, 68, 121, Snyder, 96, Snyder Junior and Senior High Schools, 96, Sunburg, 97, Sunnyside, 98, SW Gary, 99, "The Victor", 25, Victory, 107, Twombley, 68, 102, Union, 103, Upper Wildcat, 104, Valley View, 105, Wandel, 108, Welcome Hollow, 108, Weldon, 108, Weldon Valley, 109, West Nile, 110, White Building (Snyder), 96, Wildcat, 111, Willet, 111, Williams, 68, 114, Work, 115, Unidentified Schools, 115

Index

Italics denotes illustration

School Board President, Brush, 68
School Sites in Morgan County, 25
School Superintendent, 7, 64
Searles, Miss, 64
Simpson, Joyce, 107
Smith, Charles H., 121
Smith, D, 120
Smith, George, 120
Smith, Molly, 120
Smith, 68, 121
Smith, T.J., 120
Snyder Brick Building , 96
Snyder, Helen Underwood, 1914, 17
Snyder Consolidated School District, 96
Snyder, 96, *96*
Snyder Junior and Senior High Schools, 96
Snyder School District #1, 58
Sod Schoolhouse, 81, 83
South Platte River, 31
South Prairie Style, 3
Southward, Walter, 61
Stabio, Maggarino, 27
State Register of Historic Buildings, 72, 81, 92
Sunburg School, 97
Summer school receiving, 7
Sunnyside School, 98, *98*
Superintendent of Morgan County Schools, 123
Swanson, Nellie, 120

T

Teacherage, 4, 40
Teacher contract, 1920's, *14*, 15
Teacher's examination in Morgan County, 9
Teaching Certificate, Type (Class) Three, 9, 21
Teaching Diploma 90-91
Thelma Downing, 21
Tennant, Thomas, 56
"The Victor", 25
Third class teacher, 7
Thomas, Cliff, 107
Twombley School, 68, 102, *102, Cover*
Twombley, Hurd, 102, *102*

U

Underwood, Helen, 17
Union Pacific Railroad, 96
Unidentified Schools, 115
Union School, 103, *103*
University of Northern Colorado, 22
Unkown Morgan County School 18
Unkwown School Interior 99-100
Upper Wildcat School, 104, *104*

V

Valley View School, 105
Victory School, 107, *107*

Index

Italics denotes illustration

W

Walks, Ella, 56
Wandel School, 108
Warner, Margaret Louise, 90-91
Welcome Hollow School, 108
Weld County School District #4, 7
Weldon School, 108
Weldon Valley School, 109, *109*
West Nile School, 110
Wetzbarger, Mamie, 64, 120
White Building (Snyder), 96
Whittington, Mrs., 78
Wiggins Community Park, 29
Wiggins Historical Group, 81
Wiggins Historical Society, 92
Wiggins School Children on an Outing 108-109
Wiggins, Oliver, 110
Wildcat School, 111
Williams, Jack, 114
Williams School, 68, 114, *114*
Willet School, 111
Work School, 115
Works Progress Administration (WPA), 67
Word War II, 77